SPIRITOLOGY 101

Understanding Spirit, Soul, and Body

SPIRITOLOGY 101

Understanding Spirit, Soul, and Body

Dr. Jim Kaseman

Spiritology 101: Understanding Spirit, Soul, and Body
ISBN 0-9785748-0-X
Copyright © 2006 by Dr. Jim Kaseman
Published by AFCM International
P.O. Box 1918
Willmar, MN 56201

FOREWORD

As I read the manuscript for Jim Kaseman's book, *Spiritology 101*, I was reminded of a question I had asked the Lord years ago. I remember being troubled about seeing quite a bit of carnality in the lives of several Christians. I remember thinking, *Lord, your people should be further along spiritually than they are in some of these areas.* I wasn't trying to be judgmental and was mindful that I wasn't perfect either, but I recollect standing at the bathroom mirror (I was shaving at the time) and saying, "Lord, why are there so many carnal Christians?"

I guess we shouldn't be shocked when the Lord actually answers our questions! After all, the Holy Spirit has been sent to be our Teacher, our Guide, our Counselor, and the One who will lead us into all Truth! However, I was surprised (pleasantly) when some phrases leapt up in my heart that brought me illumination and understanding. The Holy Spirit seemed to answer my question about the reason for carnality among Christians with these thoughts: undeveloped spirits, unrenewed minds, and uncontrolled flesh.

Spiritual growth doesn't occur in a vacuum. It happens as we feed our spirit on the Word of God and then act on it, when we renew (not remove) our minds with His Word, and present our bodies to Him as living sacrifices. Our bodies are the temples of the Holy Spirit, and we are to present the members of our bodies as instruments of righteousness unto Him. It is only then that we'll truly grow up in Him!

I have respected and appreciated Jim and Kathleen Kaseman for many years. They have dedicated their lives to helping ministers, building churches, and expanding the kingdom of God. They are godly, sincere people with solid convictions and unwavering determination. As you read *Spiritology 101*, I believe that you'll be challenged to step into a stronger walk in the Lord than ever before, one that is Word-based, Spirit-led, and love-dominated. It is this kind of relationship with God that will enable you to experience the spiritual fulfillment and maturity that God has planned for you!

—Tony Cooke

ACKNOWLEDGEMENTS

My love and gratitude to the following:

For you Lord Jesus, for loving me before I loved you.

To Kathleen, my dear wife, friend and partner in life. Thank you for your determination to have a wonderful marriage and a close family. I am so thankful to the Lord for bringing you into my life.

Thank you Desiree, Annette, Tisha, Jonathan, and Daniel for your commitment to the Lord, family, and ministry. Your mother and I are blessed with the best children.

I will be forever grateful to Kenneth E. Hagin. The Lord used him in a mighty way to teach me how to walk with my Lord, rightly divide His Word, and be led by the Spirit.

Thank you Greg and Vicki Volich for making this book possible.

TABLE OF CONTENTS

Introduction

Spiritology, or the study of spirit, soul, and body, is one of the most important fundamental truths for born-again Christians. Getting a clear understanding of the difference between your spirit, soul, and body will enable you to better hear the voice of the Holy Spirit. You will be able to recognize when God is speaking to your heart, or when you are being led by your intellectual reasoning, or by the cravings of your flesh.

Without the understanding of spiritology, Christians can read their Bibles and ministers can preach the Word of God on a soulish level without any spiritual understanding. The Word of God is filled with a lot of good principles, such as "be kind to one another" and "do unto others as you would have them do unto you." However, when a minister preaches nice motivational messages that appeal to your soul and only cause you to become excited intellectually or emotionally, no spiritual change takes place. Eventually, when the excitement wears off, you are in exactly the same position. If change is to be lasting, it must first take place in your spirit. When your spirit being changes, then your mind and body will follow suit.

When I attended Rhema Bible Training Center in 1974, Rev. Kenneth E. Hagin always talked about doing a course on Spiritology.

However, during the time that I was in school and even after I graduated in 1975, as far as I know, he never devoted an entire course to the subject. Over the years, I have often thought of spiritology and how important it is for the body of Christ to get an understanding of spirit, soul, and body.

Being a graduate of Rhema, my ministry has followed in the footsteps of my spiritual father, Kenneth E. Hagin, in that the cornerstone of what I have preached over the past 30 years has been faith and how to be led by the Spirit of God. Of course, being led by the Spirit and living by faith go hand in hand. You cannot walk in the Spirit unless you walk by faith and vice versa. The two are tied together.

To understand faith and being led by the Spirit, you *must* have a revelation of spiritology. I am reminded of the many times I have heard Brother Hagin say, "If you don't have a revelation of spirit, soul, and body, you will never fully understand the Scriptures." How true that is.

I have noticed that when some Christians hear a minister preach a message, they do not understand how to apply what was taught to their personal lives. They *try* to do what was preached, but the results are often "hit or miss." Sometimes their faith works, but often it does not.

This is like a hunter who hears geese flying overhead, runs outside, and begins shooting up in the air, hoping to hit something. Sometimes he does, but most of the time he does not. It's like "shooting in the dark." The same is true when you try to operate in faith without understanding spiritology—most of the time, it doesn't work.

Unfortunately, many Christians spend much of their lives stumbling around hoping their faith will work instead of knowing how to make it work. God does not want us to live this way. He wants us to fully understand how spiritual things work.

We know how to follow a recipe when cooking. For example, if you are baking a cake, you mix together the ingredients in a bowl, transfer the batter into a cake pan, and put it in the oven. In about 45 minutes, you will have a delicious, moist cake. You will always get the same results when you follow the recipe.

In the same way, there are certain things you can do to assure that your faith works all the time. This begins by understanding that you are a spirit being. Brother Hagin often said, "The Bible is primarily addressed to the human spirit." Jesus said in John 6:63, *"...The words that I speak to you are spirit, and they are life."* You cannot understand spiritual things using your natural, physical senses. This is confirmed by what the Apostle Paul said in 1 Corinthians 2:14, *"the natural man does not receive the things of the Spirit of God, for they are foolishness to him: nor can he know them, because they are spiritually discerned."*

Many Christians, and even ministers, get into error because they do not discern between the natural and the supernatural. They major on eating healthy foods and exercising their physical bodies, but they do not have a clue about feeding or exercising their human spirit. It is important to develop your spirit being because it is only through being strong spiritually and understanding spiritual things that you will be able say like the Apostle Paul, *"I have fought the good fight, I have finished the race, I have kept the faith"* (2 Tim. 4:7).

Because we live in physical bodies in a physical dimension, most people are mainly focused on the physical and intellectual realms. They seldom, if ever, think about the spirit realm. Unfortunately, this applies to Christians as well. Too many believers have devotions in the morning but do not think about or talk to God for the rest of the day.

In reality, the spirit realm should be more real to us because we are spirit beings. We are part of the spiritual family of God and belong to the spirit dimension. Compared to eternity, we will only be on the earth for a short period of time. While we are here, we are commanded to walk in the Spirit (Gal. 5:16).

I believe the reason most Christians do not walk in the spirit is simply because they do not know how. Hosea 4:6 says, *"My people are destroyed for lack of knowledge...."* It is because of their lack of knowledge that they are continually "shooting in the dark," trying anything to get their faith to work. As you gain an understanding of spiritology, you will learn how to clearly recognize the voice of the Holy Spirit and understand how to purposely get your faith to work.

It is important to note that as you begin walking in the spirit, it is easy to start out doing things right but then get off and begin doing goofy things. Often, people do not even know they have done this. You have to be filled with the Word of God and be honest with yourself to discern when you have slipped into the soulish realm.

Satan manifests himself as an angel of light (2 Cor. 11:14) and counterfeits the way the Holy Spirit operates. That is why somebody can say, "The Holy Spirit told me to do such and such," and it was not the Holy Spirit speaking at all. He listened to something that was counterfeit because he could not distinguish between his spirit, soul, and body. Understanding spiritology will enable you to recognize which part of you is speaking.

I like to pray the Pauline prayers every day.

> *17[For I always pray to] the God of our Lord Jesus Christ, the Father of glory, that He may grant you a spirit of wisdom and revelation [of insight into mysteries and secrets] in the [deep and intimate] knowledge of Him, 18By having the eyes of your heart flooded with light, so that you can know and understand the hope to which He has called you, and how rich is His glorious inheritance in the saints (His set-apart ones).*
>
> Ephesians 1:17-18 AMP

This is God's will for your life. He wants you to have a deep understanding of His Word and of spiritual things. Another Pauline prayer I pray daily is found in Philippians 3:10 AMP. It says:

> *[For my determined purpose is] that I may know Him [that I may progressively become more deeply and intimately acquainted with Him, perceiving and recognizing and understanding the wonders of His Person more strongly and more clearly], and that I may in that same way come to know the power outflowing from His resurrection [which it exerts over believers], and that I may so share His sufferings as to be continually transformed [in spirit into His likeness even] to His death, [in the hope].*

The key to walking in the Spirit is getting to know God, and my desire is that you develop a closer, more intimate relationship with Him. Throughout my many years of ministry, I have seen Christians who knew God's laws and principles but did not know God. They were busy majoring on principles to get healed, to get money, to get cars or houses, instead of focusing on getting to know God.

My prayer for you is that as you gain a deeper knowledge of spiritology, you will better hear the voice of the Holy Spirit and develop a deeper relationship with your heavenly Father.

Everybody is on different levels of his or her Christian walk. Some have known the Lord for many years while others are just beginning their life with God. Regardless of how long you have known the Lord, I recommend that you read this book as though you have never heard anything about spiritology. I promise you that you will learn something new. Revelation is progressive. You may have heard teaching along this line—or if you are a minister, you may have even taught it yourself—but if you are open to the Holy Spirit, He will show you something that you have not seen before, something that will be the key to what you are looking for.

1

YOUR EARTH SUIT:
THE PHYSICAL BODY

"...may your whole spirit and soul and body be preserved blameless at the coming of our Lord Jesus Christ."
1 Thessalonians 5:23

We see from the above scripture that you are a three-part being. Notice the order that Paul listed the three parts: spirit, soul, and body. You are first and foremost a spirit being. The spirit man is the real you. It is the human spirit that communicates with the Holy Spirit.

Secondly, you have a soul. This is where your personality is, where your emotions are, and where your reasoning takes place. Your soul houses your consciousness, or your personal identity, which includes your attitudes and beliefs. Then finally, you have a physical body, which I like to call your "earth suit." Your body enables you to live and operate in this physical world as a human spirit.

To further show that you have inward and outward parts, let's look at 2 Corinthians 4:16:

> *Therefore we do not lose heart. Even though our*

outward man is perishing, yet the inward man is being renewed day by day.

The Apostle Paul specifically talks about both an outward and an inward man, showing the multi-dimensional makeup of a human being. Second Corinthians 4 continues:

> *[17]For our light affliction, which is but for a moment, is working for us a far more exceeding and eternal weight of glory, [18]while we do not look at the things which are seen, but at the things which are not seen. For the things which are seen are temporary, but the things which are not seen are eternal.*
>
> vs. 17-18

When you look at verse 18, you also see that the things of the spirit realm are eternal and the things in the physical realm—including your physical body—are temporary. While it's becoming more common for people to live 70 to 100 years and beyond, it is nothing compared to eternity.

Over the centuries, some have searched for a fountain of youth that would allow them to live for eternity. Our physical bodies, however, will not last forever. Although your physical body returns to the dust of the earth you—as a human spirit—will live for eternity, either separated from God in hell, or in His presence in heaven.

While it may seem obvious that there is a difference between the human spirit, the soul, and the physical body, not everyone believes that he or she is a triune being. Some people feel they only have a physical body and a soul. Let's look at some scriptures that show a distinction between the human spirit and physical body.

Separating the Body and Spirit

After Jesus was crucified, Joseph of Arimathaea went to Pilate and asked for permission to remove Jesus' body from the cross for burial. John 19:38 says, *"...So he came and took the body of Jesus."* This verse specifically states that Joseph of Arimathaea took the *body* of Jesus. You see, Jesus and His physical body are two different things. Let me further explain the difference.

If you are driving your daughter to school, you would say, "I am taking little Suzie to school." You would not differentiate between Suzie and her body because Suzie's human spirit and her body are so closely woven together. The difference only becomes obvious after the human spirit leaves the body. This is evident any time you go to a funeral home and view someone who has passed on. It is easy to see that the human spirit no longer lives in the body.

Another example of the difference between your human spirit and physical body is found in Philippians. When Jesus left heaven to come to the earth, Paul tells us that He left behind all of his God privileges in heaven.

3

> [6]*who, being in the form of God, did not consider it robbery to be equal with God, [7]but made Himself of no reputation, taking the form of a bondservant, and coming in the likeness of men.*

Philippians 2:6-7

We see that when Jesus was in heaven, He was in the form of God; but when He came to earth, He took on the form of a servant. We could also say that when Jesus came to the earth, He took on the form of a human being, or a human spirit. It would have been illegal for Him to come to the earth as God. Man sinned and man would have to pay the penalty of sin.

While Jesus was on the earth, He operated the same way you and I have to operate—under the power of the Holy Spirit. He was a human spirit who came *"...in the likeness of men"* (v. 7) and operated under the anointing (Acts 10:38).

Now let's analyze Romans 6:12: *"Therefore do not let sin reign in your mortal body...."* Without having the revelation of spirit, soul, and body, you would miss a lot of places in the Scriptures that are referring to more than just your body. The word "your" in this verse is actually referring to the human spirit. When you understand that, you will see that this verse is referring to both the human spirit *and* the physical body.

Most Christians are only focused on the physical body, but this thinking is backwards. Since you are a spirit being, you should focus

4

more on you as a human spirit than on your soul or your body. As you begin to think more spiritually, you will recognize more verses in the Bible that on the surface appear to refer only to the physical body. In actuality, they are referring to both the physical body and the human spirit.

Proverbs 4:23 says, *"Keep your heart with all diligence, For out of it spring the issues of life."* The word "heart" in this verse is referring to the human spirit. It is not out of your physical heart that the issues of life flow but out of you as a human spirit. We will define "heart" as part of the human spirit later in this book.

Paul said in 1 Corinthians 9:27, *"I discipline my body and bring it into subjection...."* When you dissect this verse, it is clear that it is talking about the human spirit *and* the body. "I" is referring to you as a human spirit. The human spirit is what brings the body into subjection to the Word of God, and it is the human spirit that forces the flesh to line up with Scripture.

In his second letter to the Corinthian church, Paul writes:

> *¹It is doubtless not profitable for me to boast. I will come to visions and revelations of the Lord: ²I know a man in Christ who fourteen years ago— whether in the body I do not know, or whether out of the body I do not know, God knows—such a one was caught up to the third heaven. ³And I know such a man—whether in the body or out of the body I do not know, God knows.*

> 2 Corinthians 12:1-3

5

The "I" in these verses refers to the human spirit. Paul is saying that he could not tell whether or not he as a human spirit actually left his physical body when he went to heaven. Paul could not tell the difference because he as a human spirit and his body were so closely woven together. Unless you are attuned to spiritual things, you could have a hard time knowing what was your flesh and what was you as a human spirit.

One example of spirit and body is found in Philippians 1:22-23:

> ²²*But if I live on in the flesh, this will mean fruit from my labor; yet what I shall choose I cannot tell.* ²³*For I am hard-pressed between the two, having a desire to depart and be with Christ, which is far better.*

Again, "I" in the above verses is referring to Paul as a human spirit. He wanted to leave his physical body and go to be with Christ. Yet he knew it would be better for the body of Christ if he remained on the earth a while longer.

Finally, James shows what happens to the physical body when the human spirit leaves it.

> *For as the human body apart from the spirit is lifeless, so faith apart from [its] works of obedience is also dead.*

> James 2:26 AMP

The moment the human spirit exits a physical body, the body is dead. It no longer has life. The human spirit is what gives the physical body shape and enables it to move and function.

You need your physical body to remain in the physical dimension and finish the course God has laid out for your life. The human spirit does not need a physical body to continue living. However, it cannot remain on the earth without a body. When the human spirit leaves a physical body, it continues to live for eternity.

WHAT DOES THE HUMAN BODY LOOK LIKE?

The answer to the above question may sound pretty simple. Most people would say, "Well, get a mirror and take a look!" The only problem to that answer is that there is more to you than what you can see. Our physical body has an outside part that is easily seen, but it also has an inner part that is not readily seen without special equipment.

First Corinthians 12:14 (AMP) says, *"For the body does not consist of one limb or organ but of many."* When you say "organ," most people think of the heart, lungs, kidney, liver, and things like that. The skin, however, is the largest organ of the human body, and it is the main organ that we see.

It has not always been that easy to look inside the physical body to see what our internal organs looked like. But with the development of high tech medical devices, we are able to get a clear idea of what is going on inside of us.

In addition to organs, our physical body also has five physical senses: sight, smell, hearing, taste, and touch. It is through these senses that we obtain knowledge from the physical dimension.

Scientists who are not born again gain their knowledge through their five physical senses. They experiment and attempt to figure things out. Thomas Edison was a good example of this. He tested over 3,000 filaments before he came up with his version of the light bulb.

George Washington Carver was a little different. His main textbook was his Bible, and he relied on the Spirit of God to show him things. He was known as a man who talked to flowers, and the Holy Spirit would reveal their secrets to him.

The best way for scientists to make new discovers is to learn how to rely on the Holy Spirit to show them the secrets of life instead of trusting in their five physical senses. John 4:24 says, *"God is a Spirit: and those who worship Him must worship in spirit and in truth."*

When you commune with God, He will answer the questions of life that you have. Too many people only rely on their physical senses. As you read this book, you will begin to understand the limitless knowledge you can acquire by tapping into the spirit realm. Since God created everything, He knows the answers to any questions you might have.

2

THE REAL YOU:
THE HUMAN SPIRIT

"...For the things which are seen are temporary, but the things which are not seen are eternal." 2 Corinthians 4:18

The word *spirit* comes from the Greek word *pneuma* and means "the immaterial or invisible part of man." Even though the word *immaterial* is used in the definition, don't get the idea that it is referring to something that is not real. The physical realm came out of the spiritual realm. It was created by God who is an eternal being.

The above scripture shows us that the physical realm, or what we can see, is only temporary; and the things we cannot see are eternal. The average person would not agree with this because he is firmly planted in the physical realm. He believes that what he can feel, see, and touch is reality. This is because spiritual things are not a part of his life. However, spiritual things are true reality. Unfortunately, many people are not even aware that they are a human spirit.

Have you ever given thought to what your human spirit might look like? It is not hollow but has a definite form. In fact, your spirit looks a lot like your physical body. It has eyes through which it sees and a tongue through which it speaks. If it has eyes and a tongue, it is only natural to assume that it must also have a head. And if it has a head, it must have a body.

In the *New King James Bible*, Proverbs 18:8 says that the words of a talebearer *"...go down into the inmost body."* The *King James Version* translates this phrase as the *"...innermost parts of the belly."* The word *belly* comes from the Hebrew word, *beten* and means "womb, inner body, and the seat of mental faculties." We see then that not only does your physical body have an inner part, but also an inner being, which is you as a human spirit that dwells in the physical body.

There are several scriptures in the Old Testament that reference the belly as part of the human spirit. Let's begin by looking at Proverbs 18:20 (KJV), *"A man's belly shall be satisfied with the fruit of his mouth."* The *Amplified Bible* translates *belly* as "a man's moral self."

Another verse where *belly* is referred to as part of the human spirit is Proverbs 20:27 (KJV). *"The spirit of man is the candle of the Lord, searching all the inward parts of the belly."* The word "belly" in this verse comes from the same Hebrew word, *beten*, found in Proverbs 18:20.

Psalm 139:13 says, *"You formed my inward parts...."* In the Hebrew, the phrase *"inward parts"* comes from the word *kilyah,* which means "kidney." While that may sound obscure to you, one of the definitions for *kidney* is "the seat of emotion and affection."

It is symbolic of your desires and emotions. It is interesting to note that the kidneys of bulls and goats were offered up on the altar of sacrifice in the Old Testament.

There is also reference to an inward man and a physical man in Luke 11:40: *"Foolish ones! Did not He who made the outside make the inside also?"* We see here that God created man with an inward man, or spirit being, and the outward man, or physical body. This is very obvious in 2 Corinthians 4:16, which states, *"We do not lose heart. Even though our outward man is perishing, yet the inward man is being renewed day by day."*

Finally, Paul talks about the *"hidden man of the heart"* in 1 Peter 3:4 (KJV). The human spirit is hidden in a physical body. It is clothed with flesh. That is why Paul called it the hidden man of the heart.

LAZARUS AND THE RICH RULER

We can gain insight into what the human spirit looks like from the story of Lazarus and the rich ruler.

> *[19]There was a certain rich man who was clothed in purple and fine linen and fared sumptuously every day. [20]But there was a certain beggar named Lazarus, full of sores, who was laid at his gate, [21]desiring to be fed with the crumbs which fell from the rich man's table. Moreover the dogs came and*

licked his sores. ²²So it was that the beggar died,
and was carried by the angels to Abraham's bosom.
The rich man also died and was buried. ²³And being
in torments in Hades, he lifted up his eyes and saw
Abraham afar off, and Lazarus in his bosom.

²⁴Then he cried and said, "Father Abraham,
have mercy on me, and send Lazarus that he
may dip the tip of his finger in water and cool
my tongue; for I am tormented in this flame."
²⁵But Abraham said, "Son, remember that in your
lifetime you received your good things, and likewise
Lazarus evil things; but now he is comforted and
you are tormented. ²⁶And besides all this, between
us and you there is a great gulf fixed, so that those
who want to pass from here to you cannot, nor can
those from there pass to us.

Luke 16:19-26

We see in verse 22 that Lazarus and the rich man died, and their physical bodies were buried. You will note, however, that they as human spirits continued to live even after their bodies were buried. Lazarus, the beggar, was carried to Abraham's bosom (v. 22) while the rich man was taken to Hades (v. 23).

When the Apostle Paul was caught up to heaven, he wrote in 2 Corinthians 12:2 that he could not tell whether or not he had left his body. Like Paul, I believe that when Lazarus and the rich man died, neither one of them had any idea that they were separated from their

12

physical bodies.

The rich man was in torments in hell, but it says that he saw Abraham and Lazarus afar off (v. 23). He was tormented and thirsty. He called out and heard Abraham's reply (vs. 24-25). The rich man still had his senses (sight, taste, hearing). We see from these verses that in addition to your physical body having five physical senses, your spirit being also has the same five senses (Hebrews 5:12-14).

I believe that because we are so one with our flesh, we sometimes have difficulty distinguishing between our flesh and us as a spirit. It is by renewing our minds to the Word of God that the human spirit is able to differentiate between our physical senses and our spiritual senses.

It is of utmost importance to understand that the real you is a human spirit—a human spirit that has eyes, ears, a mouth, stomach, liver, kidneys, brain (mind), etc., which are covered with flesh. This enables us, as human spirits, to operate in this physical world (Job 10:11). Adam and Eve were to produce spiritual children (eternal beings) for God and because they were to live in this physical world, they were clothed with flesh—a physical body (John 4:24, Genesis 1:26, II Corinthians 4:16-18, II Cor. 5:1-8).

FOOD FOR YOUR HUMAN SPIRIT

In the same way that your physical body needs food so does your human spirit. The type of food that newborn Christians need is found in 1 Peter 2:2: *"As newborn babes, desire the pure milk of the word, that you may grow thereby."* Paul is talking about spiritual, not physical, food.

Like young children, there comes a time when baby Christians need to stop drinking milk and begin eating meat.

> *[12]For when for the time ye ought to be teachers, ye have need that one teach you again which be the first principles of the oracles of God; and are become such as have need of milk, and not of strong meat. [13]For every one that useth milk is unskilful in the word of righteousness: for he is a babe. [14]But strong meat belongeth to them that are of full age, even those who by reason of use have their senses exercised to discern both good and evil.*
>
> Hebrews 5:12-14 KJV

These verses are not talking about physical food and drink. They are talking about food for the human spirit. As you study the Word of God, you are feeding your spirit being. The more you "eat" the Word, the more spiritually mature you will become. Some Christians are weak spiritually because they have not taken the time to read and meditate on the Word and act upon it.

Back in the seventies, I used to hear preachers say that as you feed on the Word of God, you could train your physical senses to discern good and evil. However, the more revelation I received on spirit, soul, and body, the more I realized that this was not true.

These verses in Hebrews are not talking about the physical body; they are talking about the human spirit.

I am sure you have heard people say that they have "picked up," or "sensed," things spiritually about another person. Many have thought that they could "physically" pick up on spiritual things, but that is not the case. They are really sensing things in the spirit as a human spirit. You cannot tap into the spirit realm through the physical realm, because nothing physical can cross over into the spiritual realm.

As you develop as a human spirit, you will become more sensitive to spiritual things. That is why you can meet someone for the first time and sense that something is not right. They may be sweet, quote the Bible, and say all the right things, but an evil spirit is influencing their actions.

The way you develop as a human spirit is by developing an intimate relationship with God. When you spend time with the God of the universe, you will quickly pick up on something that is contrary to His Word and His ways. It is much like bank tellers who spend so much time handling "real" money that they immediately recognize a counterfeit bill.

PHYSICALLY REACTING TO DEMONIC MANIFESTATIONS

As you develop your spiritual senses to discern good and evil, coming in contact with the spirit realm may affect you physically. I have had this happen to me. When you come in contact with a demon, although you may not see it, your flesh can react to its presence. For instance, a spirit of fear can make your hair stand on end. We see an example of this in the Old Testament when Eliphaz had an encounter with an evil spirit.

> *[14]Fear came upon me, and trembling, which made all my bones to shake. [15]Then a spirit passed before my face; the hair of my flesh stood up.*
>
> Job 4:14-15

Although Eliphaz couldn't see this spirit, he felt it. He sensed the demon in his human spirit, and his flesh reacted to its presence.

A person who is not born again but who is interested in spiritual things, can also develop his human spirit. Psychics, witches, and people who dabble in the occult are examples of this. A lot of times they talk about love and say that they see a beautiful light. What they are actually seeing and communicating with is an angel of light—a demon imitating an angel of God (2 Cor. 11:14). Eventually, when the demon has a strong grip on them, it will show its true colors and begin tormenting them. By that time, it is hard for the person to get out from its control without the intervention of a born-again

Christian who takes authority over the demon in Jesus' name.

This is how psychics can tell people whom they have never met before things that have happened in their past. Familiar spirits— spirits who are familiar with that individual—talk to them. Nothing about this is godly. It is a counterfeit of the word of knowledge. As Christians develop an intimacy with God, they will be able to discern what is and what is not of God.

Motivational speakers have also tapped into this principle. They speak positively about themselves and their future and teach others to do the same. Some of them are not born again, but they are applying godly principles to their lives and are having great results.

Just think of the things you can accomplish as a born-again Christian by developing as a human spirit. You have the advantage because the Spirit of God is dwelling inside of you. The more you grow spiritually, the more sensitive you will be to the Holy Spirit's leadings. You may be set to go one way and be checked in your "heart" to wait a few minutes or go a different way. As a result, you are spared from tragedy.

The Holy Spirit can show you things about your children, your co-workers, or people in your church. As you take the time to pray for them, their lives will be dramatically changed for the better. What an impact you can make in the lives of others simply by understanding and developing as a human spirit.

3

EVERYTHING BEGINS WITH A SEED

"The kingdom of God is as if a man should scatter seed on the ground...." Mark 4:26

In the Word of Faith circles, ministers often talk about the universal law of sowing and reaping. If you look closely at the way God operates, you will see that everything He does begins with a seed. The principle of seed time and harvest is outlined for us in Mark 4:26-29.

> *26The kingdom of God is as if a man should scatter seed on the ground, 27and should sleep by night and rise by day, and the seed should sprout and grow, he himself does not know how. 28For the earth yields crops by itself: first the blade, then the head, after that the full grain in the head. 29But when the grain ripens, immediately he puts in the sickle, because the harvest has come.*

While these verses talk about physical seed, there is also seed in the spiritual realm. Jesus said in John 6:63, *"...the words that*

I speak to you, they are spirit, and they are life." God's Word is spiritual seed, and it is planted in your heart. In the same way that a natural physical seed will grow when it is planted, the Word of God will also grow in the heart of a human spirit and produce spiritual fruit.

Galatians 3:14 states: *"That the blessing of Abraham might come upon the Gentiles in Christ Jesus, that we might receive the promise of the Spirit through faith."* God did this through a seed.

> *Now to Abraham and his Seed were the promises made. He does not say, "And to seeds," as of many, but as of one, "And to your Seed," who is Christ.*
>
> Galatians 3:16

The scripture continues:

> *And if you are Christ's, then you are Abraham's seed, and heirs according to the promise.*
>
> Galatians 3:29

After Abraham proved his obedience to God by his willingness to offer Isaac as a sacrifice, God promised to multiply and bless his descendents:

> *[17]That in blessing I will bless thee, and in multiplying I will multiply thy seed as the stars of the heaven, and as the sand which is upon the sea shore; and thy seed shall possess the gate of his enemies; [18]And in thy seed shall all the nations of the earth be*

blessed; because thou hast obeyed my voice.

Genesis 22:17-18

Notice that the word "seed" in these verses is referring to Jesus, Abraham's descendants, and anyone who enters into the kingdom of God through the redemptive work of Christ.

IN THE BEGINNING...

Now, let's go back to the book of beginnings and see how God created the earth and the purpose of seed.

¹¹Then God said, "Let the earth bring forth grass, the herb that yields seed, and the fruit tree that yields fruit according to its kind, whose seed is in itself, on the earth"; and it was so. ¹²And the earth brought forth grass, the herb that yields seed according to its kind, and the tree that yields fruit, whose seed is in itself according to its kind. And God saw that it was good.

Genesis 1:11-12

Then, on the fifth day...

²⁰God said, "Let the waters abound with an abundance of living creatures, and let birds fly above the earth across the face of the firmament of the heavens." ²¹So God created great sea creatures and every living thing that moves, with which the waters abounded, according to their kind, and

every winged bird according to its kind. And God
saw that it was good. ²²And God blessed them,
saying, "Be fruitful and multiply, and fill the waters
in the seas, and let birds multiply on the earth."

Genesis 1:20-22

When most people read these verses, they believe that God filled the ocean with fish, the sky with birds, and the earth with all of the different animals. However, I am proposing that God only created one set—a male and a female—of every species. He then commanded them to "multiply." We also see this in His creation of man.

²⁶Let Us make man in Our image, according to
Our likeness; let them have dominion over the fish
of the sea, over the birds of the air, and over the
cattle, over all the earth and over every creeping
thing that creeps on the earth. ²⁷So God created man
in His own image; in the image of God He created
him; male and female He created them.

Genesis 1:26-27

Adam and Eve were spirit beings who were created in the image and likeness of God, who is a spirit. Like the rest of creation, God only created one man and one woman and told them to "multiply."

Then God blessed them, and God said to them,
"Be fruitful and multiply; fill the earth and subdue
it; have dominion over the fish of the sea, over the

birds of the air, and over every living thing that
moves on the earth."

Genesis 1:28

God then told them to have dominion over His creation. I also propose to you that it was not Adam's physical body that had dominion over the earth. It was Adam, the human spirit, who was to rule and reign. God created man so He would have a family. He wanted someone to fellowship with, and He wanted someone who would rule and reign with Him for eternity.

This entire process was repeated after God destroyed the earth with the flood during Noah's life. When God told Noah to build the ark, He told him to bring two of all living creatures into the ark.

¹⁹And of every living thing of all flesh you shall
bring two of every sort into the ark, to keep them
alive with you; they shall be male and female. ²⁰Of
the birds after their kind, of animals after their
kind, and of every creeping thing of the earth after
its kind, two of every kind will come to you to keep
them alive.

Genesis 6:19-20

After the flood, these two animals of every kind replenished the earth. How? Through seed.

The Spirit Clothed in Flesh

To have dominion on the earth, you must have a physical body. God used the dust of the ground to create a body for Adam, the human spirit, and then placed him in the garden, eastward in Eden (Genesis 2:7-8).

We get a clear picture from the book of Job of how God clothed man's human spirit with flesh.

> *⁸Your hands have formed me and made me...*
> *⁹Remember [earnestly], I beseech You, that You have fashioned me as clay [out of the same earth material, exquisitely and elaborately]. And will you bring me into dust again? ¹¹You have clothed me with skin and flesh and have knit me together with bones and sinews. ¹²You have granted me life and favor, and Your providence has preserved my spirit.*
>
> Job 10:8-9, 11-12 AMP

When Job said that God had *"...formed and made him..."* in verse 8, he was really talking about himself as a human spirit. This is also true in verse 11. The word "me" refers to the human spirit. Verse 11 can be translated, "You have clothed *me as a human spirit* with skin and flesh." Skin and flesh is the earth suit that God gave to every human spirit. And finally, in verse 12 he said, *"...Your providence has preserved my spirit."* We can see in these verses a clear distinction between the spirit and the flesh of man.

Fearfully and Wonderfully Made

When you look at the human body and the intricate way in which God made it, you have to agree with the writer of Psalm 139—you are wonderfully made.

> ¹³*For You formed my inward parts; You covered me in my mother's womb.* ¹⁴*I will praise You, for I am fearfully and wonderfully made...."*
>
> Psalm 139:13-14

Looking at these verses without understanding spirit, soul, and body, you would not realize that it is not talking about the physical body but about the human spirit.

The phrase "inward parts" in verse 13 is referring to the human spirit. We see from this verse that God formed the human spirit and then covered it with flesh. It is at the moment of conception—when a sperm and the egg unite—that the human spirit instantly becomes intertwined with flesh.

When a fetus is aborted, not only is a developing physical body aborted; but more importantly, a developing human spirit is also aborted.

This also brings up another point. Some would believe that there are baby human spirits hovering around the throne of God waiting for Him to send them to the earth. This cannot be true because it violates the seed and harvest principle. It is when the seed of a man and woman unite that the human spirit begins to form.

Everything begins with a seed.

It is important to recognize the three-dimensional aspect of our makeup. When we quit focusing on the physical realm and set our sights on learning how to tap into the spiritual dimension, not only will we be able to better understand Scripture, but we will also make better decisions because we are truly being led by the Spirit of God.

4

Your Inner Self:

The Soul

"For the word of God is living and powerful, and sharper than any two-edged sword, piercing even to the division of soul and spirit...." Hebrews 4:12

The soul is the consciousness, or awareness, of your identity, or inner self. It is where your personality, behaviors, and attitudes are, and where your mental faculties, or intellect, reside. The soul is developed through your experiences and through formal education.

In Chapter 2, we saw how the human spirit was clothed with flesh, or the physical body. In the same way, the brain is the physical clothing for the soul. The brain's cerebral cortex, which contains a complex neural network, along with the enteric nervous system which line the belly of the human spirit, makes up the soul of man.

One of the best ways to describe the function of the soul is with the word *interface*, which means "the point where independent and often unrelated systems meet." The soul resides in the brain and is the interface where information is exchanged between the human spirit and the body. The soul makes it possible for the human spirit to communicate with the flesh and the flesh to communicate with the spirit.

Many people think the spirit and soul are the same thing, but they are two separate entities. Part of the reason people think this is because the two words are often used interchangeably throughout the Bible. You have to read the context of the Scripture to be able to tell if the verse is talking about the soul or the spirit. An example of this is found in the Apostle Peter's letter to Christians scattered throughout Asia Minor. When talking about the flood, Peter said that *"...eight souls were saved through water"* (1 Peter 3:20). He was actually referring to human spirits here. Their entire beings were saved—the human spirit clothed in flesh, along with the soul, or intellect.

The Fall of Man

The fall of man came through the soul. Satan used knowledge to tempt and deceive Eve. He said in Genesis 3:5, *"God knows that in the day you eat of it your eyes will be opened, and you will be like God, knowing good and evil."* Eve acted on the temptation, believing that she would become like God if she ate the fruit. We know from 1 Timothy 2:14 that Adam was not deceived. He was fully aware that what the devil told Eve was a lie, but he stood by and allowed her to eat the fruit.

As a result of Adam's disobedience and the fall of mankind, the human spirit became dead spiritually and the soul became a slave to the flesh. Satan then gained control of the earthly realm and became god of this physical dimension. He is the god of the world system, and he appeals to the five physical senses, or the flesh, to get to the soul. If he can get to your soul, he can ultimately get into your heart.

Even though we live in a physical world, God has given us weapons to combat Satan's method of operation. Paul shows us how to win the battle between the flesh and the soul in 2 Corinthians 10:3-5:

> *3For though we walk in the flesh, we do not war according to the flesh. 4For the weapons of our warfare are not carnal but mighty in God for pulling down strongholds, 5casting down arguments, and every high thing that exalts itself against the knowledge of God, bringing every thought into captivity to the obedience of Christ.*

It is when you dwell on wrong thoughts that the devil is able to gain entrance into your soul. However, when you cast down thoughts that are contrary to the Word of God, you gain supremacy over the devil.

An example of this is worry. The more you dwell on negative thoughts, the bigger that situation appears. By casting down thoughts of worry and instead focusing on what the Word says, you gain supremacy over the attacks of the devil.

THE ANIMAL VS. THE HUMAN SOUL

Animals have a soul, but they do not have a spirit. They have emotions and some memory. For instance, you can train dogs to do tricks, as well as to protect you. When you look at circus animals, you see that even wild animals can be trained. God has primarily wired animals to act instinctively. In other words, the thinking has already been done for them. Animals in the feline family, for example, are predators. All types of felines from lions to household cats have a natural instinct to hunt.

The human soul, on the other hand, is completely different. Unlike animals, the soul of the human spirit reasons, comprehends, and gathers knowledge. The human spirit with the soul is also creative.

When the human spirit leaves the physical body, the soul goes with it. If a human physical body could live without a spirit, it would not be any different than an animal. It would act and react to situations by instinct rather than by reasoning.

THE SPIRIT AND THE SOUL

The Bible is filled with references regarding the soul, the first of which is found in Genesis 2:7 (KJV), *"And the Lord God formed man of the dust of the ground, and breathed into his nostrils the breath of life; and man became a living soul."* The word "soul" refers to Adam's entire being—spirit, soul, and body.

God commanded us in Deuteronomy 6:5 to *"...love the Lord your God with all your heart, with all your soul, and with all your strength."* Again, the word "soul" in this verse refers to your entire being—your spirit, soul, and body. In Psalm 16:10, we see that only the human spirit is referred to. *"For you will not leave my soul in [hell]...."* When you die, your physical body remains on the earth. Only you as a human spirit, along with your soul, goes to heaven or hell.

Another verse that only refers to the human spirit is Psalm 19:7, which states, *"The law of the Lord is perfect, converting the soul...."* Your human spirit is what becomes born again. Your thinking and your actions change after your human spirit is recreated. Psalm 23:3 begins by saying, *"He restores my soul...."* This verse is talking about all three parts of your being—your spirit, soul, and body.

The above verses are all from the Old Testament. The revelation of the triune nature of man did not come until after Jesus was born. We do not really get a clear revelation of spirit, soul, and body until we look into the New Testament, with 1 Thessalonians 5:23 being the primary text. *"...and may your whole spirit, soul, and body be preserved blameless at the coming of our Lord Jesus Christ."*

There are several other verses where it is understood that the words "you" or "I" refer to the human spirit.

> *¹I beseech you therefore, brethren, by the mercies of God, that you present your bodies a living sacrifice, holy, acceptable to God, which is your reasonable service. ²And do not be conformed to this world, but be transformed by the renewing of your mind, that you may prove what is that good and acceptable and perfect will of God.*
>
> Romans 12:1-2

31

"You" in verse 1 refers to the human spirit. It is you, the human spirit, who presents your body to God. The mind is the soulish part of man, and it is up to the human spirit to dominate it. We also see in 1 Corinthians 9:27 that the human spirit is responsible for bringing the body under subjection: *"But I discipline my body and bring it into subjection...."* "I" refers to the human spirit. We see in these three verses of scripture, the differentiation of spirit, soul, and body.

The better you are able to distinguish between your spirit and your soul, the better you will be able to recognize the difference between the reasoning of your mind and the still, quiet voice of the Holy Spirit. This is important when making decisions, as our goal is to always follow the voice of the Holy Spirit who speaks to our spirit. By doing so, we will always make the right decisions and avoid many pitfalls in life.

5

SEPARATING THE HEART AND MIND

"Then I will raise up for Myself a faithful priest who shall do according to what is in My heart and in My mind...." 1 Samuel 2:35

God is saying in 1 Samuel 2:35 that He will raise up someone who will be faithful to do what is in His heart and mind. We see from this verse that God, the Ultimate Spirit, has a heart and mind. If God, who is a spirit, has a heart and mind, it is reasonable to believe that since we were created in His image, our human spirits also have hearts and minds.

There is also a scripture reference in the New Testament that shows that the human spirit has a heart and mind. Notice that the word "your" in verse 6 is referring to the human spirit.

> *[6]Be anxious for nothing, but in everything by prayer and supplication, with thanksgiving, let your requests be made known to God; [7]and the peace of God, which surpasses all understanding, will guard your hearts and minds through Christ Jesus.*
>
> Philippians 4:6-7

According to the *Merriam-Webster's Dictionary, heart* means "breast or bosom; the emotional or moral as distinguished from the intellectual; the central or inmost part." One of the definitions for *breast* is "the seat of the emotions and thought." The "bosom" refers to the chest, and the chest is conceived of as the seat of the emotions and intimate feelings.

Following are several scriptures that refer to the heart of the human spirit:

> *A happy heart is good medicine and a cheerful mind works healing, but a broken spirit dries up the bones.*
>
> Proverbs 17:22 AMP

> *...incline your ear to wisdom, and apply your heart to understanding.*
>
> Proverbs 2:2

> *A calm and undisturbed mind and heart are the life and health of the body....*
>
> Proverbs 14:30 AMP

> *Keep and guard your hearts with all vigilance... for out of it flow the springs of life.*
>
> Proverbs 4:23 AMP

When the heart is referred to as the "central and inmost part," the translators often use the word "belly." Scriptures referring to the belly include:

> *He who believeth on me, as the scripture hath said,*
> *out of his belly shall flow rivers of living water.*
>
> John 7:38 KJV

The *Amplified Bible* translates John 7:38 as, *"...From his innermost being shall flow [continuously] springs and rivers of living water."* This verse is referring to the human spirit. The forces of life do not come from the human body; they come from the human spirit.

Another reference for "belly" is found in Proverbs 18:8 (KJV): *"The words of a talebearer are as wounds, and they go down into the innermost parts of the belly."* The Hebrew word for *belly* in this verse is *beten* and refers to "the inmost being of a person." "Belly" here refers to the heart of the human spirit.

The *King James Bible* translates Song of Solomon 5:4 as, *"My beloved put in his hand by the hole of the door, and my bowels were moved for him."* The word "bowels" is referring to the heart. The *New King James Version* says, *"...my heart yearned for him."* Though it does not sound very romantic, the writer of the Song of Songs was saying, "I love you with all of my bowels."

THE DWELLING PLACE OF THE HEART

We see from the previous verses that your heart, or belly, resides in the center of your being. Let's look at a familiar passage to further show the location of the heart of your human spirit.

...if you confess with your mouth the Lord
Jesus and believe in your heart that God has raised
Him from the dead, you will be saved. For with the
heart one believes unto righteousness, and with the
mouth confession is made unto salvation.

Romans 10:9-10

When you say, "I believe with all my heart," do you grab your head? No. Do you grab your chest, where your physical heart is? No. You grab your abdomen, or your gut. So, like the writer of Song of Songs, you could say, "I believe with all of my bowels (or heart)." That is where your faith is—in your heart, or in your belly.

You believe unto righteousness in your heart, not your head. What do you do in your head? You renew your mind to the Word of God and cast down wrong thoughts (2 Cor. 10:5). You believe in your heart, not in your mind. Have you ever heard someone say, "I had a 'gut' feeling about that"? The person was picking up something in his heart, or inner most being.

What he was feeling is also scientific. Doctors have learned from studying the body that there are nearly 100 million nerve cells in your "gut," or abdominal area. If you have ever become nervous and it felt like your stomach was fluttering, the nerve cells in your abdomen were reacting to your situation.

Medical researchers are now saying that we have two brains. Of course, we are all familiar with the one encased in our skull, but the lesser known brain is entrenched throughout our abdominal area and is called the "enteric nervous system."[a]

Where does the Holy Spirit speak to you? In your gut or heart, not in your head or mind. However, your heart and your head or mind do communicate with each other through a very long neural cable called the "vagus nerve."

When I learned how the brain and the gut communicate with each other, I was immediately reminded of how Brother Hagin often taught that your heart knows things that your mind doesn't know. God speaks to your heart first and then that information is transferred to your mind. Christ dwells in our heart (Eph. 3:17). The Holy Spirit dwells in our hearts (I John 4:4, John 7:38-39).

We have known and have taught for years how to be led by the Holy Spirit and how to hear the voice of the Spirit of God. For too long, however, we have only looked at our body as a physical being, but it is much more than a one-dimensional entity. When you study the human body and see how many nerves and neurotransmitters there are in your spinal cord, abdominal region, and the brain, you will see how God wired you as a human spirit so that you can recognize when the Holy Spirit is speaking to you.

[a] Taken from The Maker's Diet by Jordan S. Rubin. Copyright © 2004 by Jordin S. Rubin, N.M.D., Ph.D. Used by permission of Zondervan, www.zondervan.com.

Agreeing With Your Mind and Heart

After ministering on spiritology one time, the pastor of the church gave me an interesting nugget. He read Matthew 18:19, which says, *"Again I say to you that if two of you agree on earth concerning anything that they ask, it will be done for them by My Father in heaven."* The Lord showed him that this scripture could also be applied to your mind and heart. When your mind and heart agree, anything you ask shall be done for you.

I think he's on to something. The Apostle Paul instructs us to renew our minds (Rom. 12:2). As our mind agrees with God's Word, we have our mind and heart working together. When the soul and the heart are controlled by the Holy Spirit, you will not have any problem keeping your flesh under control and receiving what you are believing for.

However, when the soul dominates the flesh, then you have born-again Christians who have gotten themselves into some real messes. In their hearts, they didn't want to do what they did—and this can range from overeating, to drugs and alcohol, to having an affair—but their flesh dominated their actions. Now they are in trouble up to their eyeballs because their soul and their flesh were in harmony!

I have had many people sit across from my desk over the years looking for counseling, and the counsel that I have given time and time again is to "follow your heart." When you follow your heart, you will always do the right thing. When you follow your flesh, or the reasonings of your mind, you will get in trouble.

Now that we are able to recognize the difference between spirit, soul, and body, instead of ignoring the "gut" feelings that we have, we can confidently make the right decisions by following our hearts.

6

Classification
of Human Spirits

*"And I, brethren, could not speak to you as to spiritual people but as to
carnal, as to babes in Christ."* 1 Corinthians 3:1

It is through the soul and the flesh that Satan is able to deceive
mankind. The devil has been around from before the creation
of man and has been able to watch us for eons. As a result, he
knows how we think and act. He also knows how God works.
One of his methods of deception is to transform himself into an
angel of light (2 Cor. 11:14) and appeal to our natural senses to
counterfeit the way the Holy Spirit operates. He imitates the pure
life of the Spirit of God and tricks Christians into thinking that
they are being led by the Holy Spirit and are walking by faith when
they are not.

Problems arise for many Christians because they are not able
to separate the soulish and spiritual realms. They do not recognize
the true leading of the Holy Spirit versus the false, devilish leadings
through their senses.

To better understand the dividing of spirit and soul, let's first
look at the different classes and maturity levels of human spirits.

Saved and Unsaved / Mature and Immature

Human spirits fall into two classes: those who are children
of the devil and those who are children of God (I John 3:10). The
children of the devil are what we call "natural men." These people
are spiritually dead because they have not made Jesus Christ the
Lord of their lives. However, the moment they receive the free gift
of salvation and become new creations in Christ, they enter into the
class of human spirits who are called Christians.

Christians can be further divided into four classes. First, there is
the spiritual Christian. This is a person who is dominated by the Holy
Spirit. In other words, the Spirit of God indwells and energizes this
human spirit. We could say that Jesus is truly Lord of him—spirit,
soul, and body. The Holy Spirit is able to work through his spirit and
then through his soul. When the Holy Spirit has complete control of
the spirit and soul, then that human spirit can dominate the cravings
of the human body, or flesh.

Keep in mind that God works through the spirit, soul, and body.
Satan works in the opposite manner: through the body, soul, and
spirit. The devil cannot posses a human spirit without first gaining
control of a person's mind and body. He entices you through your
flesh or your soul to eventually get to your spirit.

Secondly, there is the soulish Christian who is dominated
by his soul (his mind, reasonings, and intellect). This person is
also energized by his flesh. The Holy Spirit is more or less pushed
aside, and the individual is controlled by his intellect and emotions.

This is the type of person who is constantly questioning. He does not understand the things of the Spirit because he is trying to intellectualize God and the way He works.

A soulish person can also be governed by his emotions. He is the type of person who is on fire for God one day and on the verge of backsliding the next. He is moved by whatever is happening around him.

Have you ever seen preachers who scream and shout and work up a sweat when they preach? More than likely, they are preaching out of their soul and flesh. They are trying to "work" things up in the congregation. There is a danger when ministers do this because they open themselves up to wrong spirits. It is important to guard against trying to "feel" the presence of God in the soulish realm.

In the same way, Christians should not try to "work" things up in the natural either. "Pushing" for an angel to show himself in the physical realm or demanding that God manifests Himself in a spectacular way opens you up to evil spirits who are all too willing to accommodate you. If God *chooses* to manifest Himself or if God permits an angel to appear, that is wonderful. But remember, it is up to God, not you.

Thirdly, the carnal Christian is dominated by the flesh, and his actions can also manifest through the soul. The desires of the flesh are listed in Galatians 5:19-21. They include idolatry, selfishness, division, dissensions, drunkenness, adultery, fornication, etc. You name the sin, and it is included in this list. It can be hard for the

Holy Spirit to get through to the carnal Christian. The Holy Spirit speaks in a still small voice, and this person is used to the voice of the flesh, which screams.

And finally, baby Christians are often selfish and fall into the soulish, or carnal categories. In the same way that a newborn baby only thinks of himself, it is natural for someone who is newly born again to act selfishly. Many young Christians do and say things that cause more mature believers to shake their heads. They are just too young in the Lord to know any better, and it takes time for them to renew their minds to the Word of God.

In the same way that a baby develops into a toddler and learns not to be selfish, so must a babe in Christ. All Christians need to grow out of the babyhood stage and become spiritual Christians. There are two scriptures in the New Testament that refer to babes in Christ. Let's look first at 1 Peter 2:2: *"As newborn babes, desire the sincere milk of the word, that ye may grow thereby."* The word "babes" in this verse means an infant, or a new baby.

The other scripture reference is found in 1 Corinthians.

> *¹And I, brethren, could not speak unto you as unto spiritual, but as unto carnal, even as unto babes in Christ. ²I have fed you with milk, and not with meat: for hitherto ye were not able to bear it, neither yet now are ye able. For ye are yet carnal: ³for*

whereas there is among you envying, and
strife, and divisions, are ye not carnal, and
walk as men?

1 Corinthians 3:1-3 KJV

The word "babes" in 1 Corinthians 3:1 comes from a different Greek word. It means "someone who is childish in nature." In other words, this is a person who is not a baby but is acting like one.

I am sure you have come across a person like this. If you would check his driver's license, you would see that he is 40 years old. However, the way he is throwing a "fit," you would think that he is only three months old. He should have grown up a long time ago, but he is still acting like a baby.

Romans 8:14 says, *"For as many as are led by the Spirit of God, these are the sons of God."* The word "sons" in this verse refers to someone who is a mature Christian. A son of God is someone who dominates his physical body and soul and allows the Holy Spirit to have free reign in his life.

An immature Christian is someone who is controlled by his circumstances. He bases his decisions on his five physical senses— what he feels, sees, tastes, smells, and touches. He intellectualizes the situation and makes decisions based on his reasonings. He doesn't understand spiritual things because he is controlled by his intellect and flesh.

Animation of the Soul

45

I once read literature written by some of the old theologians who were talking about the "animation of the soul." To *animate* means "to give life to; to give motion to; to inspire." When cartoons first came out, they were hand drawn. Later, when they were animated for film, the illustrator would sketch hundreds of drawings, each showing a slightly different movement. Then, when the pages were flipped rapidly, it seemed as though the character moved.

The soul is animated from one of two sources. Old theologians called it the "lower" life and the "higher" life. The soul can be animated—or given life—by either the Spirit of God, which is the higher life, or through the lower life, which is also called the animal life. It is interesting that theologians used the term "animal life," because if a human physical body could live without a spirit, it would not be any different than an animal. It would operate by instinct and could not be led by the Spirit of God because the Holy Spirit did not dwell in this body.

On the other hand, when you are animated by the Holy Spirit, the fruit of the spirit is evident in your life. Your life will be filled with love, joy, peace, patience, kindness, goodness, faithfulness, gentleness, and self-control (Gal. 5:22). When you as a human spirit begins to manifest the fruit of the spirit, your soul and flesh eventually follow suit as you bring your soul and flesh in subjection to the Word of God (I Cor. 9:27, Rom. 12:1-2).

In time, your soul will no longer be able to dominate you. Instead, you will be spirit dominated. Then you will be true spiritual men and women who know the difference between your spirit and soul and are able to walk in the Spirit all of the time.

7

DIVIDING
THE SPIRIT AND SOUL

*"I, the Lord, search the heart, I test the mind, Even to give every
man according to his ways, According to the fruit of his doings."*
Jeremiah 17:10

In this chapter we will examine four soulish areas that often
trip Christians up and cause them to follow after their souls
rather than the Word of God. The first area deals with *soul
affections,* or *soul relationships.*

> *[32]Therefore, everyone who acknowledges Me
> before men and confesses Me [out of a state of
> oneness with Me], I will also acknowledge him
> before My Father Who is in heaven and confess
> [that I am abiding in] him. [33]But whoever denies
> and disowns Me before men, I also will deny and
> disown him before My Father Who is in heaven.
> [34]Do not think that I have come to bring peace upon
> the earth; I have not come to bring peace, but a
> sword. [35]For I have come to part asunder a man*

from his father, and a daughter from her mother,
and a newly married wife from her mother-in-
law-- 36And a man's foes will be they of his own
household. 37He who loves [and takes more pleasure
in] father or mother more than [in] Me is not
worthy of Me; and he who loves [and takes more
pleasure in] son or daughter more than [in] Me
is not worthy of Me; 38And he who does not take
up his cross and follow Me [cleave steadfastly to
Me, conforming wholly to My example in living
and, if need be, in dying also] is not worthy of
Me. 39Whoever finds his [lower] life will lose it [the
higher life], and whoever loses his [lower] life on
My account will find it [the higher life]..

Matthew 10:32-39 AMP

In looking at verse 39, a problem arises with the way the verse was translated. The translators wrote: *"He who finds his life...."* The Greek word for *life* is *psuche* and means "soul life." In the *Worrell New Testament*, a footnote appears by the word "life," noting that the Greek translation for this word is *soul*. The verse should actually read, "He who finds his *soul* will lose it, and he who loses his *soul* for My sake will find it."

You may wonder how you can lose your soul; and once you lose it, how you find it again. You lose your soul by yielding to the lower animal life instead of the higher life, which is being led by the Spirit. Soul affections, or soul relationships, will keep you from yielding to the Spirit of God. I have seen this many times throughout my years of ministry.

I heard a grandparent once say, "God told my daughter and her husband to go Africa. They can't go to Africa! If they do, I know I will never see my grandchildren again." This attitude can stop a lot of people from going to the mission field. Instead of being obedient to God, they are yielding to the desires and soul relationships of their families.

I have also known people who have delayed going into the ministry because they wanted to wait until their children graduated from high school. Have you ever stopped to think about what you are communicating to God when you do things like this? You are saying that you love your family more than you love Him. You are willing to be led by your family but not by God.

Romans 8:14 says, *"For as many as are led by the Spirit of God, these are the sons of God."* This verse does not say that you are led by your teenagers or by their grandparents. Putting family relationships before God is yielding to the lower life. If you do this, you will lose your soul. In other words, you will step out of God's will for your life and open yourself up to the devil.

The Amplified Bible makes this point very clear in Matthew 10:39: *"Whoever finds his [lower] life will lose it [the higher life], and whoever loses his [lower] life on My account will find it [the higher life]."* In this verse, *higher life* means "eternal life." If you find your soul, you are going to lose eternal life.

ABRAHAM'S OBEDIENCE; ELI'S DISOBEDIENCE

Abraham is an example of someone who put God before his family. When God told him to offer up Isaac, he immediately obeyed. As a result, he made a way for the Savior to be born and for all of mankind to be saved (Gen. 22:1-14).

On the other hand, Eli, the priest, is an example of someone who put his children before God. Eli did not train his sons up in the ways of the Lord. They treated the offering of the Lord with contempt; they ate food they were not supposed to eat, and they had sexual relations with women who came to the temple. However, Eli would not correct his sons, and they continued to sin before God (1 Sam. 2:12-17, 22-25).

God was angry with Eli and said to him, *"Why do you kick at My sacrifice and My offering which I have commanded in My dwelling place, and honor your sons more than Me, to make yourselves fat with the best of all the offerings of Israel My people?"* (1 Sam. 2:29). Eli, however, never enforced God's commandments in his own house. As a result of his soul affection for his children, both of his sons died on the same day. A curse was also placed on his family and all of his descendents died in the prime of their lives (vs. 31).

Any time you love and honor your family or another person more than God, you will lose them. Matthew 10:34 says, *"Do not think that I came to bring peace on the earth. I did not come to bring peace but a sword."* Following after Christ can be like a sword that divides your family, as they may disagree with what God is telling you to do and try to keep you out of the will of God.

A PERSONAL TIME OF TESTING

In my own life, I had an opportunity to put God's will before the desires of my family. Some of our children are adopted. When our youngest son came into our lives, he had been in an abusive situation and needed short-term care.

We had not planned to adopt any more children. However, after Danny came into our home, the Lord spoke to my wife and said that he had been brought to us to raise. We were living in Minnesota and assumed that we would be there until he was 18. When Danny was about four years old, the Lord began to deal with us to move our ministry to Oklahoma.

The only problem with obeying God in this situation was that we would have to leave Danny behind. He was a foster child and a ward of the state of Minnesota. To make matters worse, the judge in the county where we lived had a reputation of never allowing foster parents to adopt a child if they knew the parents. Well, I used to pastor the parents.

We made up our minds, though, that we were going to obey God. We announced to our church that we were moving to Tulsa. We also told the social workers our plans, and they began looking for a new home for Danny. To make a long story short, in less than 30 days we were standing before a judge; and instead of Danny being taken away from us, he legally became our fifth child.

I know if we had told the Lord that we could not move to Tulsa for another 14 years, things would not have worked out well for us. You can rest assured, that if you always put God first, He will make a way when there seems to be no other way.

Soulish Self-Interest

The second soulish area to guard against is also found in the book of Matthew and deals with soulish self-interest.

> *24Then Jesus said to His disciples, If anyone desires to be My disciple, let him deny himself [disregard, lose sight of, and forget himself and his own interests] and take up his cross and follow Me [cleave steadfastly to Me, conform wholly to My example in living and, if need be, in dying, also]. 25For whoever is bent on saving his [temporal] life [his comfort and security here] shall lose it [eternal life]; and whoever loses his life [his comfort and security here] for My sake shall find it [life everlasting]. 26For what will it profit a man if he gains the whole world and forfeits his life [his blessed [b]life in the kingdom*

of God]? Or what would a man give as an
exchange for his [blessed] life [in the kingdom of
God]?

Matthew 16:24-26 AMP

Jesus is telling us to deny ourselves in these verses. In the *Amplified Bible*, verse 24 reads, *"...If anyone desires to be My disciple, let him deny himself [disregard, lose sight of, and forget himself and his own interest]...."* As we had seen in Matthew 10:39, the word "life" in verse 25 also should have been translated "soul."

Other words that describe self-interest include: self-preservation, self-pity, and self-centeredness. All of these words are based in selfishness. Instead of pouring your life out to others as you are instructed to do, you are consumed with your own wants and desires. To combat this, you must *"...deny [yourself], and take up [your] cross daily, and follow [Christ]..."* (Luke 9:23).

The works of the flesh listed in Galatians 5:19-21—adultery, fornication, indecency, hatred, contentions, jealousy, outbursts of wrath, selfish ambitions, envy, drunkenness, etc.—are all actions of someone who is consumed with his or her own self-interest.

Self-interest also involves self-preservation. An example of this is when you try to cover up a mistake you have made. You do this because you are afraid of what might happen if people found out what you did. I have seen this in the ministry. People have covered up their mistakes because they are afraid they will lose their ministry.

Sometimes they will even continue in a wrong direction, because they do not want people to know they have missed it.

A pastor can operate in soulish self-interest when taking up an offering. For example, the building payment is due, and he knows the funds are not where they need to be. Instead of trusting God, he puts pressure on the congregation by hammering them and making them feel condemned if they don't give. He is not trusting God to bring in the money. He is operating in a soulish area because of his own fears and selfishness. What the pastor doesn't realize is that if he continues to operate like this, people will leave his church.

Soulish self-interest can also dominate families. The root of any abusive relationship is self-interest. The offending person is only concerned about him or herself. True love is more concerned about the other person and his or her wants and desires.

The way to combat selfishness is found in Philippians.

> ³*Do nothing from factional motives [through contentiousness, strife, selfishness, or for unworthy ends] or prompted by conceit and empty arrogance. Instead, in the true spirit of humility (lowliness of mind) let each regard the others as better than and superior to himself [thinking more highly of one another than you do of yourselves]. ⁴Let each of you esteem and look upon and be concerned for not [merely] his own interests, but also each for the interests of others.*

Philippians 2:3-4 AMP

Instead of being consumed with self-interest, spend your time thinking about the interests of others. Begin walking in love. How do you do that? Start by reading and meditating on 1 Corinthians 13, the love chapter. Read it in *The Amplified Bible.* It will change the way you think and cause you to be more concerned about others instead of yourself. You will also notice that your faith will work better, because faith works by love.

SOULISH GRASPING FOR EARTHLY THINGS

The third area of dividing the spirit and the soul is what I call the "soulish grasping for earthly things." This involves trying to hold on to earthly things instead of laying down your soulish desires and following after God. To better understand this soulish area, let's look at the story of Lot's wife.

You will remember that two angels came to Sodom to deliver Lot and his family from the impending destruction of Sodom and Gomorrah. After the angels had taken them out of the city, they instructed Lot's family to flee for their lives and not look back (Gen. 19:16-17). As you know, Lot's wife did look back and was turned into a pillar of salt (Gen. 19:26).

Look at what Jesus said about this incident.

> *32Remember Lot's wife. 33Whosoever shall seek to gain his soul shall lose it; but whosoever shall lose it will preserve it.*
>
> Luke 17:32-33 WORRELL

A.S. Worrell commented that if you seek to save your soul—meaning your physical life, or your unrenewed mind that is controlled by the physical things in life—by disobeying God's commands, you will ultimately lose it.

"Soulish grasping for earthly things" is an area where we can disobey God's command and lose our soul because we are putting earthly things before God. Don't get me wrong. It is God's will for us to prosper, not only spiritually but financially and materially as well. However, we are to seek the kingdom of God first and then these things will be added to us. We are to always worship God. *He* is our gold and silver (Job 22:25).

When God brought the Israelites out of Egypt, He gave them wealth. But He warned them in Deuteronomy to never forget where the wealth came from.

> *[11]Beware that you do not forget the Lord your God by not keeping His commandments, His judgments, and His statutes which I command you today, [12]lest—when you have eaten and are full, and have built beautiful houses and dwell in them; [13]and when your herds and your flocks multiply, and your silver and your gold are multiplied, and all that you have is multiplied; [14]when your heart is lifted up, and you forget the Lord your God who brought you out of the land of Egypt, from the house of bondage.*

> Deuteronomy 8:11-14

You see, disobedience comes when God is no longer first place in your life. If He didn't want the Israelites to have wealth, He could have delivered them from Egypt with nothing but the clothes on their backs. He did not do that. Now that they were going into the Promised Land, He was warning them not to let money become their god.

Following are some examples of how people can grasp for earthly things today. Some old-time Pentecostal preachers had a three-point message they called "Gals, Gold, and Glory." Another way to say this is "sex, money, and pride." These are the three most common sins that Christians commit. They involve themselves in sexual sin; money becomes their god; and they become full of pride.

I want to specifically look at money. We see that Jesus had some warnings about riches.

> *15And He said to them, "Take heed and beware of covetousness, for one's life does not consist in the abundance of the things he possesses." 16Then He spoke a parable to them, saying: "The ground of a certain rich man yielded plentifully. 17And he thought within himself, saying, 'What shall I do, since I have no room to store my crops?' 18So he said, 'I will do this: I will pull down my barns and build greater, and there I will store all my crops and my goods. 19And I will say to my soul, "Soul, you have many goods laid up for many years; take your ease; eat, drink, and be merry."' 20But God said*

to him, 'Fool! This night your soul will be required
of you; then whose will those things be which you
*have provided?' *[21]*"So is he who lays up treasure for*
himself, and is not rich toward God."

Luke 12:15-21

This parable shows us that when you focus on getting wealth and material possessions and leave God out of your life, you will end up with nothing.

People who do not understand spiritual things have used these verses to say that riches are sinful. However, if you look at Haggai 2:8, you see that the silver and the gold belong to God. In Psalm 50:10, we learn that the cattle on a thousand hills belong to Him as well. If having riches is a sin, then God is the biggest sinner in the universe, because He owns everything.

Let's continue reading what Jesus had to say:

[22]Then He said to His disciples, "Therefore I
say to you, do not worry about your life, what you
will eat; nor about the body, what you will put on.
[23]Life is more than food, and the body is more than
clothing. [24]Consider the ravens, for they neither sow
nor reap, which have neither storehouse nor barn;
and God feeds them. Of how much more value are
you than the birds?

[29]"And do not seek what you should eat or what
you should drink, nor have an anxious mind. [30]For

all these things the nations of the world seek after,
and your Father knows that you need these things.
³¹But seek the kingdom of God, and all these things
shall be added to you."

Luke 12:22-24, 29-31

Jesus is still talking about everything that is in the rich fool's barn. He did not change subjects in the middle of his teaching. Notice that He said in verses 30 and 31 that God knows you need these things. If you will only seek Him first, everything you need will be added to you.

We have a choice to make. We can seek after the riches and lose God (eternal life), or we can seek after God and let Him add the riches to our lives. Do you remember what it says in Deuteronomy 30:19? *"...I have set before you life and death, blessing and cursing; therefore choose life that both you and your descendants may live."* God is letting us know that the way we choose will make the difference between life and death. What will your choice be?

I am also reminded of the story of David. After he had the affair with Bathsheba and learned that she was pregnant, he concocted a plan to cover up his sin. He had her husband, Uriah, sent to the front lines of the war to make certain he would die in battle. He thought his plan to hide what he did was successful. However, the Spirit of God showed the prophet Nathan everything. The prophet came to David and said, *"I gave you your master's house, and your master's wives into your keeping, and gave you the house of Israel and of*

Judah. And if that had been too little, I would have given you much more" (2 Sam. 12:8).

God is saying here that He would have given David anything he wanted. He did not have to do such despicable things. It is in the heart of God to bless us with wealth and finances. He simply wants us to put Him first in our lives.

Soulish Self-Love

The fourth area that we need to guard against is soulish self-love. This is being full of love for yourself. It's all about *me—my* family, *my* things, *my* way. Self-love is being selfish, and selfishness is satanic. It has destroyed more churches and marriages than you can shake a finger at.

Selfish people are controlled by fear, which is Satan's nature. First John 4:18 says, *"There is no fear in love; but perfect love casts out fear, because fear involves torment. But he who fears has not been made perfect in love."* Fear prevents you from walking in the fullness of God.

When you look at what happened in the Garden of Eden, you can see that Adam sinned for selfish reasons. The first thing he said to God after he sinned was *"...I was afraid, because I was naked; and I hid myself"* (Gen. 3:10).

Selfish people are always afraid. They have a fear that they won't get promoted. They think they should be getting more compliments than the other person. They wonder why something was done for another person but not for them. They lie awake at night tormented, thinking that they should have had this or that.

They are controlled by fear, and fear keeps them from walking in the fullness of what God has for them. Since they are bound by fear, they are especially careful about stepping out to do what God has instructed them to do. They are too afraid to get out of the boat and walk on water. What is their pathway to freedom? It is found in 2 Corinthians 5:14-15 (AMP):

> *14For the love of Christ controls and urges*
> *and impels us, because we are of the opinion and*
> *conviction that [if] One died for all, then all died;*
> *15And He died for all, so that all those who live*
> *might live no longer to and for themselves, but to*
> *and for Him Who died and was raised again for*
> *their sake.*

We have been purchased with the blood of Christ, so we should no longer live for ourselves but for God. Our spirit and our body do not belong to us anymore (1 Cor. 6:19-20). We are not here to do what we want to do but what He wants us to do.

If you operate in the soulish realm, your focus is only on yourself. However, as you renew your mind, you will begin thinking like the Word of God. Once the Spirit of God has control of your human spirit, then your soul will come in subjection to your spirit. You will be like Jesus in the Garden of Gethsemane and say, "...

nevertheless not My will, but Yours, be done" (Luke 22:42). This should be our attitude in everything we do.

The weapons that God has given you to battle soulish areas are mighty. You can be victorious over selfishness by casting down imaginations and every high thing that exalts itself against God (2 Cor. 10:4-5). Even though you cannot stop Satan from firing thoughts into your mind, you can cast them down before they become strongholds. What you want is for God's Word to become a stronghold in your soul. As you renew your mind, which is part of the soul, then your heart and your soul will agree with each other.

Luke 21:19 (KJV) says, *"In your patience possess ye your souls."* We see from this verse that you can lose possession of your soul. This happens when Satan comes to you with thoughts and you yield to them instead of casting them down. You then begin meditating on his lies and eventually begin speaking words of doubt and unbelief over your life. You may want to give up because you don't have possession of your soul.

The way to counter this is to renew your mind by reading and meditating on the Word of God. You may find that you do well for a day or two and then slip back into selfishness. Don't get discouraged, but be patient. It takes time. Just keep holding fast to your confession. You will eventually come to the place where you have grown spiritually and no longer give in to the areas of self, but walk in love and do the will of God.

ABSTAINING FROM WINE AND ALCOHOL

"Now see to it that you drink no wine or other fermented drink...." Judges 13:4 NIV

It is so important to be able to differentiate between your human spirit, soulish areas, and the physical body. Christians who are not able to do this often get themselves into a lot of trouble. They may think that they are being led by the Holy Spirit, when actually, they are giving in to the reasonings of their minds or following after their fleshly desires.

Wine and any type of alcoholic beverage are things that hinder your ability to tell the difference between your spirit, soul, and body. When most people think of wine, they automatically think of a beverage that contains alcohol. However, in the Middle East and in ancient culture, wine also meant freshly squeezed juice from fruit without alcohol. When reading the Bible, you have to look at the context of the verses to discern whether the passage is talking about wine with alcohol or grape juice that has not fermented. The word "wine" (Gk *oinos*) in the New Testament is a generic term that can refer to either fermented wine or unfermented wine. The nature of *oinos* must be determined by the context and likelihood.

While there is nothing wrong with drinking juice made from grapes, the Scripture has some strong words about alcoholic beverages. In the book of Leviticus, God gave Aaron the following instructions regarding any fermented drink.

> *⁹Do not drink wine or intoxicating drink,*
> *you, nor your sons with you, when you go into the*
> *tabernacle of meeting, lest you die. It shall be a*
> *statute forever throughout your generations, ¹⁰that*
> *you may distinguish between holy and unholy, and*
> *between unclean and clean.*
>
> Leviticus 10:9-10

Alcohol alters your mental faculties because it is a drug. Verse 10 states that you will not be able to *"...distinguish between holy and unholy, and between unclean and clean."* In other words, you won't be able to tell right from wrong. Alcohol hinders your ability to tell what is from God and what is from the devil.

The prophet Isaiah also had strong words for ministers who drank.

> *But they also have erred through wine, And*
> *through intoxicating drink are out of the way;*
> *The priest and the prophet have erred through*
> *intoxicating drink, They are swallowed up by wine,*
> *They are out of the way through intoxicating drink;*
> *They err in vision, they stumble in judgment.*
>
> Isaiah 28:7

Alcohol caused these priests and prophets to err in vision and stumble in judgment. Many don't realize that alcohol not only affects your physical body, it also affects you as a human spirit. It keeps you from being able to tell the difference between physical input and spiritual input.

Satan wants to keep you in the physical dimension so he can feed you religious lies and false doctrine. Unfortunately, because wine and alcohol keep you focused on physical things, you will believe his lies and act on them, thinking the entire time that you are hearing from God.

I know preachers who believe it is okay to drink wine with alcohol. They base their beliefs on the account in John 2:1-11 that tells the story of Jesus turning water into wine at a wedding in Cana. However, it would have been impossible for Jesus to turn water into wine with alcohol. If He had, He would have sinned against God by contributing to a drunken party and would not have been able to go to the Cross of Calvary. However, according to various ancient writers, the "good" (choice, or best) wine was the sweetest wine—i.e., one that could be drunk freely without the fear of intoxication. It is significant that the Greek adjective translated "good" here is not *agathos*, meaning "good," but *kalos*, meaning "morally excellent or befitting."

Priestly Separation From Alcohol

Looking at Ezekiel 44:21, you will see that it says, *"No priest shall drink wine when he enters the inner court."* Today, we could add to that verse and say that no priest will drink wine, smoke marijuana, snort cocaine, or shoot heroin! Alcohol is no different than any of these other drugs. They all alter your mental faculties. Take a look at what Proverbs says about wine.

> *31Do not look on the wine when it is red,*
> *When it sparkles in the cup, When it swirls around*
> *smoothly; 32At the last it bites like a serpent, And*
> *stings like a viper. 33Your eyes will see strange*
> *things, And your heart will utter perverse things.*
> Proverbs 23:31-33

Alcohol affects your heart—the belly of your human spirit and your mind—and causes you to say things you will later regret. It loosens your tongue. I am sure you have seen someone who was drunk tell anybody who would listen everything about himself and whatever else was on his mind.

I remember reading an article in the late seventies by Dr. David Yonggi Cho. He is the senior pastor of Yoido Full Gospel Church in South Korea. His church has the world's largest congregation with over a half a million members. A brain surgeon who is a member of his congregation shared with him some of his research regarding the speech control center of the brain. The surgeon discovered that when you speak, your body sends out signals to different parts of your body. For instance, if you say, "I'm tired," signals are sent throughout your body to prepare your body to go to sleep.

What does this have to do with drinking wine or alcohol? Verse 33 in Proverbs 23 says that alcohol causes you to "...*utter perverse things.*" Remember that Jesus said in John 6:63, "...*The words that I speak to you are spirit, and they are life.*" When you speak, your words affect both the spiritual and physical realms.

Words are spiritual. They are clothed with physical sound so you can hear them in this natural world. But your words will affect both your human spirit and your physical flesh. That is why it says in Proverbs 4:23 (AMP) to "*keep and guard your heart with all vigilance....*" When you say "I'm sick," you are allowing sickness to come on your human spirit. Sickness then manifests in your physical body.

We see how this can happen when Jesus was on the cross. Not only did He bear the sins of mankind, but all of our sicknesses and diseases were also put on His human spirit. Isaiah 52:14 says that His appearance was marred more than any man. What happened to Him in the spiritual realm affected His physical body.

Another example of this is seen in people who have had out-of-body experiences. Let's say that a person was in a bad car accident and was in a lot of pain. While the doctors were working on him in the emergency room, he died and slipped out of his body. When he entered the spirit realm, his human spirit no longer experienced the pain his physical body felt. However, when the doctors revive him and he comes back into his body, he feels the pain again.

The words that you speak affect two worlds: the physical

world as well as the spiritual world. The writer of Proverbs 23 is warning you that alcohol will cause you to speak things that will affect you negatively.

Now, let's take a look at some verses from the *Contemporary English Version.*

> *4Kings and leaders should not get drunk or even want to drink. 5Drinking makes you forget your responsibilities, and you mistreat the poor. 6Beer and wine are only for the dying or for those who have lost all hope.*

> Proverbs 31:4-6 CEV

This translation is calling you a king and a leader. You may think that this does not apply to you if you are not a minister of the gospel. You see yourself as an ordinary Christian. However, according to 1 Peter 2:9 (KJV), you are *"...a chosen generation, a royal priesthood, an holy nation, a peculiar people; that ye should shew forth the praises of him...."*

We also see in Revelation 1:6 that we have been made kings and priests unto God. We are all priests. Unlike the Old Testament priests, we are always on duty—twenty-four hours a day, seven days a week. Under the Old Testament, it was an automatic death penalty if a priest drank fermented wine and then entered the tabernacle of God. Well, you are a temple of the Holy Spirit. God Almighty lives inside of you. Tell me then, when are you not on duty?

Since we are operating under the New Testament dispensation, we won't *die* if we have a glass of wine or an alcoholic beverage. But we do not want to do anything that will hinder our ability to clearly hear the voice of God. We want to live our lives pure and holy before God and live in a way that is pleasing in His sight.

As we rapidly approach the return of our Lord Jesus, Scripture clearly outlines the events that will take place on the earth. Now more than ever, with the increase of terrorism and lawlessness, we want to be sure that our human spirit is controlling our soul and body. We cannot allow anything to get in our way of clearly hearing the voice of the Holy Spirit.

9

Developing a Strong Human Spirit

"This Book of the Law shall not depart from your mouth, but you shall meditate in it day and night...For then you will make your way prosperous, and then you will have good success." Joshua 1:8

There are specific things you can do to become strong spiritually and get your mind and heart in agreement with each other. The first step in developing a healthy, strong human spirit is found in Proverbs 4:20 which says, *"give attention to my words...."* In other words, give the Word of God first place in your daily life. In every situation you encounter, the first thing you should consider is what the Word says.

For example, let's say a child falls down the stairs and gets hurt. What is the first thing you would do? Most people would immediately call 911. However, if the Word was first place in your thoughts, you would lay hands on the child and pray first. Then you can call 911.

When you are not used to putting the Word first, you tend to exhaust everything there is to do in the natural first. When nothing seems to work, then you will call every intercessor you know across the country. And when all else fails, you begin declaring the Word of God over the situation

This method is backwards. You must put the Word to work right away. Actually, on a daily basis and before anything happens, you should be continually declaring that no weapon formed against you will prosper (Isa. 54:17) and that no tragedy will visit your household. This way you can prevent accidents and the need to call 911.

In Joshua 1:8, the word *meditate* means "to think; to ponder; to study; to mutter." Really, what you are doing when you meditate on the Word is practicing the presence of God. The Apostle John wrote in John 1:14 that the Word was made flesh. Jesus also told His disciples in Luke 24:44 that the Law of Moses, the Prophets, and Psalms were really talking about Him.

It is important to set aside time every day to read and meditate on the Word and spend time with God. Some people are morning people, while others function better at night. The important thing is to be consistent and fellowship with God every day. That way, when situations pop up in your life, you will immediately begin to speak the Word over it. This is how you grow and develop.

Food for the Human Spirit

Earlier we talked about the human spirit having a belly. We also read scripture that called the Word of God food. First Peter 2:2 calls the Scripture milk. The Word is called both milk and strong meat in

Hebrews 5:12-14 and 1 Corinthians 3:1-3. In the same way that your physical body needs physical food, you need spiritual food to feed your human spirit. Your human spirit cannot live on potatoes, gravy, and roast beef. It needs the Word of God.

A professor of language at the University of Montana told me that the word *meditate* also means "to chew the cud." Have you ever watched a cow? After the animal swallows some hay or grass, he will bring it back up and chew on it again. He gets all of the nutrition he can out of his food.

We need to do that same thing with the Word of God. We should think about the Word, talk about the Word, confess the Word, and hold fast to our confession without wavering. You "chew" the Word by talking and meditating on it.

The Emphasized Bible by J. B. Rotherham translates Joshua 1:8 like this: *"This scroll of the law must not cease out of thy mouth, but thou must talk to thyself therein, day and night...."* As we talk the Word, we hear it; and as we hear the Word, our faith is developed because faith comes by hearing (Rom. 10:17) and doing or obeying the Word of God (James 2:26).

When Proverbs 4:21 says, *"Do not let them* [the Word of God] *depart from your eyes...,"* it is talking about the eyes of your human spirit. You are to keep the Word before your eyes so you can observe to do what it says.

Many Christians have a lot of scripture memorized. However,

even if you are able to quote most of the Bible, it is still important to read the Word. Why? Because we are believing that the eyes of our hearts would be flooded with light so that we can know and understand the hope to which He has called us (Eph. 1:18 AMP).

When you are driving your car, it is important to see clearly so you don't have an accident. It is the same way spiritually. You need to be able to see clearly. God wants us to understand mysteries and secret things (Dan. 2:22; Deut. 29:29).

Observe to Do

God told Joshua to meditate on the Word so he would *"observe to do..."* (Josh. 1:8). What are we to observe to do? The answer is found in Philippians 4:9: *"The things which you learned and received and heard and saw in me, these do...."* Did you catch the three important words in this verse? Hear, see, and do. Words paint pictures. What you hear is what you see, and what you see is what you do.

You will do or be what you hear. Somebody who is constantly called "dumb" or "stupid" while growing up will believe those words. It doesn't matter that he has the highest IQ in his class. He sees himself as stupid because that is the only thing that he has ever heard. Unfortunately, because he believes what he has heard, he will do whatever it takes to look stupid.

I have known attractive women and handsome men who believed they were ugly. They only heard how ugly they were all their lives, and they believed those words. There was nothing that could be said to convince them otherwise.

When it comes to the Word of God, we need to hear it, see it, and then do it. The Word is our spiritual food. Have you ever gone to somebody's home for dinner, and the aroma of what they have cooked has filled the house? The food smells so good. But isn't it so much better to sit down and eat the food, rather than to just smell it? It is the same way with the Word of God. When we hear good preaching, we are really smelling spiritual food. You begin to eat the Word when you preach what you have heard to yourself. You develop a certain amount of faith when you listen to tapes or CDs, but your faith really soars when you speak it and then act on it.

Protecting Your Heart

In the second half of Proverbs 4:21, we are instructed to keep the Word in the midst of our hearts. Then in verse 23, we are told to protect our heart at all costs, for out of if flows the issues of life. The reason we protect our heart is so the Word that we have been speaking and sowing into our heart is not stolen from us.

We can see how the devil steals from us when we look at the parable of the sower in Mark 4:15: *"And these are the ones by the wayside where the word is sown. When they hear, Satan comes immediately and takes away the word that was sown in their hearts."* This verse is talking about people who are easily swayed from the Word of God. They hear a message on healing, but as soon as they have a symptom in their body, they throw what they have heard out the window. This can apply to any topic that is found in the Word: prosperity, peace, deliverance, etc.

There are ways, however, that you can protect the Word that is in your heart. We see in verses 14 through 20 of Mark 4 that Satan is able to steal the Word from your heart through hard times (afflictions), persecution, deceitfulness of riches, the cares and worries of the world, and lust for other things. The way that you protect your heart is by not allowing these things talk you out of the Word.

If you look at the lives of the apostles, you will see that many of them were thrown in prison at one time or another. But because they protected their hearts, prison didn't get into them. A lot of the New Testament was written by Paul while he was in prison. If he had allowed prison to get into him, he probably would not have written anything. What I am saying is that when you are hit with hard times and persecution, don't take it personally. Remember, what you are experiencing is a ploy from the devil to steal the Word from your heart.

In addition, don't allow yourself to worry. Worry is a form of meditation. When you worry, you are allowing fear to choke the Word you have heard, and it becomes unfruitful.

The parable in Mark 4 also talks about the deceitfulness of riches. When you allow God to be your gold and silver (Job 22:25), then you will not be deceived by riches. When your focus is to seek God first and allow Him to add riches to your life, then money will be in its proper perspective. It is when you major on material things instead of the Word that you allow the Word to be strangled and become ineffective.

INSTANT OBEDIENCE

Instantly obeying your heart also develops a strong, healthy human spirit. If your heart is telling you to do something, then do it. You can rest assured that if you have taken the time to meditate on the Word, when you sense the Holy Spirit is telling you to do something, you will have a firm foundation to stand on. When you are stepping out on the Word and are doing something in line with what God has promised, you won't have to call ten people trying to figure out if what you are sensing is God or not. You can confidently trust in the Word that is in your heart.

However, if you develop a habit of dragging your feet when God speaks to you, you will get to the point where you won't hear His voice. If you want to stay sensitive and tender to the things of the Spirit, then you must instantly obey His promptings. Otherwise, you will harden your heart.

John G. Lake is an example of someone who was very sensitive to the voice of the Holy Spirit. One day as he was driving down the highway, the Holy Spirit said, "Pull over to the wrong side of the road and stop." He did it without question or hesitation. Just as he had gotten to the side of the road, a truck driver, who had lost control of his vehicle, came barreling over the top of the hill on the wrong side of the road—the side that John G. Lake had been on. If he had not instantly obeyed the voice of the Holy Spirit, he would have been in the pathway of that truck and probably would have been killed. You see, you don't always have time to call somebody to ask if they think what you heard was from God or not.

James 2:20 says, "...faith without works is dead." But how do you know if you are stepping out in faith, foolishness, or presumption in your situation? The answer is learn to be led by the Spirit and allow the Holy Spirit to lead and guide you in what steps to take. You do not have to guess. Simply wait until you feel that you have the mind of the Holy Spirit and then do what He tells you to do.

Sometimes, as you are learning to hear the voice of the Spirit, both directions sound equally the same. "Yes, do this." "No, don't do that." What do you do in situations like this? Simply step out in one direction. It won't take long to figure out if you have missed it or not. If you feel you are going the wrong way after you have stepped out, quickly repent, come back to the starting point, and go in the other direction.

You have to walk in the light that you have. You can't wait until you are perfectly mature before you step out. If you make a mistake, God will forgive you. He would rather you step out and make a few mistakes than to do nothing. The more you are grounded in the Word, the better you will be able to differentiate between your spirit, soul, and body. You will be able to recognize what is coming from your soulish realm and what is coming from your heart. After awhile, it will be easy to distinguish between the two; and you will eliminate a lot of problems for yourself.

10

HOW TO BE
LED BY THE SPIRIT

"For as many as are led by the Spirit of God, they are the sons of God." Romans 8:14

The Holy Spirit guides you through the heart of your human spirit. Proverbs 20:27 says, *"The spirit of man is the lamp of the Lord, searching all the inner depths of his heart."* When this verse talks about the *"...lamp of the Lord...,"* it means that God will enlighten you or guide you through your human spirit. In the Hebrew, *inner depths* literally means "rooms, or chambers." It is referring to the rooms of the belly of the human spirit.

Brother Hagin used to say that there is a supernatural way and a spectacular way to be led by the Holy Spirit. Spectacular ways are also supernatural, but being led supernaturally means that your faith is involved in hearing the voice of the Holy Spirit. A spectacular manifestation is something that astonishes the five physical senses. The parting of the Red Sea and the angel, Gabriel, appearing to Mary, the mother of Jesus, were both spectacular manifestations.

There are three ways you can be led by the Spirit supernaturally: the inward witness, the inward voice, and the voice of the Holy Spirit. Some of the spectacular manifestations include visions—either a spiritual vision or an open vision—trances, dreams, or a word from a prophet.

Whether the Holy Spirit chooses to lead you in a supernatural or spectacular way, one thing is for certain, it will always line up with the Word of God. The Holy Spirit will never do or say anything that is contrary to the written Word. In fact, the Word of God is the standard by which you judge all things. If something is in agreement with what the Word says, it is safe to say that God is in it. However, if what you are seeing, hearing, or feeling is contrary to the Word, then toss it out. It is not of God.

You should never "push" to be led spectacularly. Doing so will only open you up to demonic manifestations. Likewise, don't seek to have angels appear to you. If you push hard enough, more than likely the devil will accommodate you. If God sees fit for an angel to appear to you or for you to fall into a trance, then let Him bring that into your life.

God wants all believers to know *His* voice. He doesn't want you to have to rely on other people to tell you what is from God and what is not. There is nothing wrong with getting input from other people, but you may not always be able to get in touch with fellow believers. Missionaries are an example of this. They can't always pick up a phone and call someone. At one time or another, you will have to make an instant decision; and you need to be able to clearly recognize the Holy Spirit's voice. If you have taken the time to listen, but for some reason are not able to discern His voice, you may use the wisdom revealed in God's Word and common sense in the matter. Just do what is right (II Tim. 4:8 AMP).

Now, let's go over the different ways the Holy Spirit will lead you.

THE INWARD WITNESS

An inward witness can be compared to intuition. It is an immediate knowing of something without the conscious use of reasoning. You just know something in your belly, or in your gut. It is not something that you have thought through in your mind. It is something that you immediately know in the heart of your human spirit. You just know if something is right or if it is wrong.

Some people call it a green light or a red light. A green light feels like peace, and you have an urge to "go for it." A red like feels like a check, or a warning not to do something.

Isaiah 55:12 says that the sons of God are led forth with peace. For me, the inward witness is primarily the peace I do or do not have. I either have peace or an uncomfortable sense in my spirit. When the Apostle Paul was a prisoner aboard a ship, he said to the crew, *"Men, I perceive that this voyage will end with disaster and much loss..."*

85

(Acts 27:10). Paul perceived something. He had an inward intuition, or an inward knowing, that something bad was going to happen. It wasn't something that he got from his natural reasonings. It was something he felt in his gut.

Another way to recognize a "red light," or a check in your spirit is if you feel like you are being pushed into doing something. The Holy Spirit never pushes. If you feel this way, then you probably should not do it. Isaiah 28:16 (KJV) says, *"...he that believeth shall not make haste."* You often hear of people who have rushed into a "good deal" that wasn't going to be around for a long time. If something is of God, it can wait. Faith does not get in a hurry when you are led by the Spirit. Timing is important when it comes to God. Sometimes you need to obey immediately; but at other times, what God wants you to do will happen over a period of time.

THE INWARD VOICE

The second way to be led by a supernatural manifestation is through the inward voice. When talking about the inward voice, we are talking about your conscience. We see this in Romans 9:1: *"I tell the truth in Christ, I am not lying, my conscience also bearing me witness in the Holy Spirit."*

Sometimes we refer to our conscience as the still, small voice of the human spirit that senses right and wrong. If you are born again, you can trust your conscience because you have the nature of God residing in you. If a person is not born again, his conscience cannot be trusted. Satan is the father of lies (John 8:44), and his nature controls those who have not given their lives to Christ.

This is why an unsaved person can look you in the eye and lie. After someone gives his life to the Lord, even if he is a young Christian, his heart pricks him when he doesn't tell the truth. It is possible, however, for a Christian to override his conscience. If he continually does this, he will come to a place where his conscience is seared (1 Tim. 4:2) and his heart becomes hardened. Then he is back to the same mess he was in before he gave his life to Christ.

Before you became born again, your conscience was defiled, as noted in Titus 1:15: *"To the pure all things are pure, but to those who are defiled and unbelieving, nothing is pure; but even their mind and conscience are defiled."* This is how someone can kill a person without remorse. His conscience is so defiled and polluted that he justifies his wrong deeds.

Unfortunately, even Christians can get to a place where they no longer listen to their conscience. The Apostle Paul calls this shipwrecking your faith.

> *Holding fast to faith (that leaning of the entire*
> *human personality on God in absolute trust and*
> *confidence) and having a good (clear) conscience.*
> *By rejecting and thrusting from them [their*
> *conscience], some individuals have made shipwreck*
> *of their faith."*

> 1 Timothy 1:19 AMP

This scripture shows that when you violate your conscience, you will end up with shipwrecked faith.

THE VOICE OF THE HOLY SPIRIT

The third of the supernatural leadings is through the voice of the Holy Spirit. The book of Acts is filled with examples of the Holy Spirit speaking to the apostles. One example is found in the book of Acts. Peter was on the rooftop praying when he fell into a trance. Afterward, when he was thinking about what he saw, the Holy Spirit spoke to him and said, *"...Behold, three men are seeking you. Arise, therefore, go down and go with them, doubting nothing; for I have sent them"* (Acts 10:19-20). Peter did as the Holy Spirit said, and found the men waiting for him.

Usually when the Holy Spirit speaks to you, His voice is much louder and more authoritative than your inward voice. Sometimes the voice of the Holy Spirit can even sound as though somebody behind you is talking. Sometimes you even want to turn around to see who is there. It almost sounds like an audible voice, but it isn't. I had that happen to me.

Before we purchased the property where our ministry in Branson is now located, I heard the Holy Spirit say, "The Father has need of that property." It sounded like somebody was standing behind me speaking.

As with your inward voice and inward witness, the Holy Spirit will never tell you anything that is contrary to the Word of God. If what you are hearing does not line up with the Word of God, then you have missed it. It is not the Holy Spirit talking.

Some people want the Holy Spirit to confirm to them in an audible voice what their conscience is telling them to do or what they are sensing through an inward witness. You do not need Him to do that, and you need to be careful about looking for voices. There are a lot of voices out there. If the Holy Spirit speaks to you, He will agree with the Word of God, with your conscience, and with your inward witness.

No Condemnation in Christ

John 16:8 says, *"when He has come, He will convict the world of sin...."* There are two words that you need to remind yourself of when thinking of the Holy Spirit. They are condemnation and conviction. These words should never be mixed up. The devil is the one who condemns, not the Holy Spirit. The devil condemns people and tries to make them think that it is really the Holy Spirit who is condemning them.

Jesus paid the penalty for our sins. His shed blood has washed away our sins, and we have been forgiven. The Holy Spirit convicts us of sin by pointing out the fact that we need a savior. He then gives us the opportunity to repent. He never condemns us.

SPECTACULAR MANIFESTATIONS OF THE HOLY SPIRIT

There are also spectacular manifestations of the Holy Spirit. The first one we will cover is visions. Probably the most spectacular vision in the New Testament is when Jesus appeared to Saul on the road to Damascus.

> *3As he journeyed he came near Damascus, and suddenly a light shone around him from heaven. 4Then he fell to the ground, and heard a voice saying to him, "Saul, Saul, why are you persecuting Me?" 7And the men who journeyed with him stood speechless, hearing a voice but seeing no one.*

> Acts 9:3-5, 7

Saul was the only person who saw the light. He saw Jesus. The people who were with him only heard a voice. This is called a spiritual vision because the men with Saul didn't see anything. It would have been an open vision if everyone with him had seen the light.

Anther incident of someone's eyes being opened is in 2 Kings. Elisha had been receiving words of knowledge about the battle plans and strategies of Israel's enemies. He would quickly reveal this information to the king of Israel who was then able to defeat the enemy. When the king of Aram learned of this, he sent his army to capture Elisha. The next morning when Elisha and his servant got up, they were surrounded by the king's army. Elisha encouraged his fearful servant by saying:

> *16"...Do not fear, for those who are with us are*

more than those who are with them." ¹⁷And Elisha
prayed, and said, "Lord, I pray, open his eyes that he
may see." Then the Lord opened the eyes of the young
man, and he saw. And behold, the mountain was full
of horses and chariots of fire all around Elisha.

2 Kings 6:16-17

The servant's eyes were open, and he saw into the spirit realm. He was able to see the multitude of angels who were doing battle on their behalf.

In Acts 8:26, we see where the eyes of Philip were opened. He had an open vision of an angel appearing to him and showing him places where he was to preach the gospel. Acts 5:19 also records an incident where Peter and the apostles had been thrown in prison because of the healings and miracles that were being done through them. An angel of the Lord appeared to them and opened the prison door, giving them instructions to continue preaching in the temple. This also was an open vision.

The Holy Spirit can also cause you to fall into a trance. Peter fell into a trance in Acts 10:9-10. He then had a vision of the Lord instructing him to eat unclean animals. As was mentioned earlier, the Holy Spirit then told him to go with the Gentiles who were waiting for him.

Your senses are suspended when you are in a trance. You are not unconscious, but you are more conscious of the spirit realm than you are of the physical realm. You might think the person is in a daze and move your hand in front of his face to see if he recognizes that you are there.

The Holy Spirit will also speak in dreams. Acts 2:17 says, *"And it shall come to pass in the last days, says God, That I will pour out of my spirit on all flesh; your sons and your daughters shall prophesy, your young men shall see visions, your old men shall dream dreams."*

Before and after the birth of Jesus, Joseph had several dreams where he received instruction from God. When he learned that Mary was pregnant, he was going to divorce her until he had a dream.

> *But while he thought about these things, behold, an angel of the Lord appeared to him in a dream, saying, "Joseph, son of David, do not be afraid to take Mary your wife, for that which is conceived in her is of the Holy Spirit.*
>
> Matthew 1:20

After Jesus was born, Joseph had another dream, warning him to get his family out of Bethlehem.

> *...behold, an angel of the Lord appeared to Joseph in a dream, saying, "Arise, and take the young Child and his mother, flee into Egypt, and stay there until I bring you word; for Herod will seek the young Child to destroy him.*
>
> Matthew 2:13

Later, when it was safe to leave Egypt, he had a third dream.

> [19]*Now when Herod was dead, behold, an angel of the Lord appeared in a dream to Joseph in Egypt,* [20]*saying, Arise, take the young Child and his mother, and go into the land of Israel, for those who sought the young Child's life are dead.*
>
> Matthew 2:19-20

Genesis 28:10-15 gives the account of a dream Jacob had. He dreamed of a stairway that connected heaven and earth. In the dream he saw the angels of God ascending and descending on the staircase. In his dream, God made a covenant with Jacob about his descendants.

God also spoke to Joseph, Jacob's son, in two different dreams, showing him that he would one day be a ruler (Gen. 37:5-9). After suffering years of slavery and imprisonment, Joseph did indeed become governor of Egypt. One day when his brothers came to him requesting grain, he remembered the dreams of his youth (Gen. 42:8-9).

A note of caution here. Not every dream a person has is an expression of guidance from the Holy Spirit. And, as with visions and trances, when the Holy Spirit speaks to you in a dream, it will line up with the Word of God; and it will bear witness with your heart.

Words From Prophets

Finally, another spectacular manifestation of the Holy Spirit is

93

when God will use prophets to speak to you. Keep in mind that we are under the new blood covenant, and the sons of God are led by the Spirit of God (Rom. 8:14). If God chooses to speak to you through a prophet, that is entirely up to Him.

I have had a prophet of God speak to me, but I do not seek after prophets for direction. All of the major decisions I have ever made started with an inward witness. When a prophet did have a word for me, it was a confirmation of what was already in my spirit. That word didn't help me so much initially, but five or ten years down the road when I was going through a difficult time, it helped to sustain me.

In the Old Testament, because the people did not have the Spirit of God in them, they had to go to a prophet for direction. That is not the case for you and me. We have the Spirit of God living on the inside of us, and He speaks directly to each of us. The best way to be led by the Spirit of God is through the inward witness. And for that, you need to be able to clearly hear the voice of the Holy Spirit.

Keep in mind that if you never have a vision or fall into a trance; if you never see an angel or hear an audible voice, you have the inward witness and the Word of God to be your guide. The Apostle Peter calls the Word *"...a more sure word of prophecy"* (2 Pe. 1:19).

11

~⚜~

MY JOURNEY OF UNDERSTANDING
SPIRIT, SOUL, AND BODY

Sometimes hearing the experiences of another person can help you better discern between the voice of the Holy Spirit, the voice of your mind, and the voice of your flesh. I want to share with you my journey of understanding spiritology. You may be able to relate to what has happened to me and be better able to distinguish between your spirit, soul, and body.

Three years after I was born again, I enrolled in Rhema Bible Training Center, which at that time was located in Tulsa, Oklahoma. One day after I came home from school, I was just so excited about the Lord that I started dancing around the living room. Suddenly, I knew I needed to get quiet.

In a moment of time, the Lord showed me why I had experienced so many problems before I gave my life to the Lord. I had a call of God on my life; and since I was out of His will, things didn't go well for me. After I gave my life to the Lord, I was still having challenges. But I knew in that moment the challenges I experienced were because I had not obeyed the call to the ministry that was on my life.

I yielded to what the Lord was showing me and said, "Okay, I'll go full time in the ministry." I also knew that I was going to start by pastoring a small church and then someday I would travel around the world teaching.

I can say this now because of what I know about spirit, soul, and body; but at the time, I didn't know this. What the Lord showed me about my calling came from my heart, but I quickly slipped from my heart and into the soulish realm of my mind. My mind said, "I'm going to have to pastor for 20 years before I can travel around the world teaching."

After I graduated from Rhema in 1975, I couldn't figure out if we should move back to North Dakota or go somewhere else. I was having a hard time finding that "small church." I heard about a full gospel church in Louisiana that needed a pastor, but I couldn't get clear direction from the Lord on whether to go to Louisiana or North Dakota. Finally, I told my wife, "Well, we're going back to North Dakota; but on the way, let's stop in Louisiana."

I believed that when I got to that particular city in Louisiana, I would know what we were supposed to do. Sure enough, as soon as we hit the city limits, it felt as though I had died and gone to hell. I felt horrible inside. I knew that I knew that I knew that I was in the wrong place.

We went to the church and ministered, and it became even more obvious that we were not supposed to be there. The people did not like us at all. They were born again, Spirit filled, and tongue talking; but they were also racists. They hated African Americans. My son is African American and Caucasian, and they were not going to have anything to do with us.

Even though the experience was horrible, we learned something from it. As soon as we crossed the city limits, we knew beyond a shadow of a doubt that we were in the wrong place.

I have often counseled people who felt they were called to the mission field to make a trip to that country before they sell everything and move their families to the middle of a jungle or a third world country. Check out how your spirit feels when you are there. You will know if you are supposed to stay or not. I have had many people thank me later. They only realized once they were there that they were not called to that country.

People often become emotional when you talk about missions, but emotions are in the soulish realm. When you see a need, learn to discern the difference between being moved by your emotions and being moved by the Holy Spirit.

HEADING NORTH

Instead of going straight to North Dakota from Louisiana, we went back to Tulsa to attend Kenneth E. Hagin's Campmeeting. At one of the services, Kenneth Hagin Jr. came up to me and asked how things were going. I told him what had happened in Louisiana, and he said, "You know, we got a letter from a church in Minnesota that is looking for a pastor." The minute he told me about that church, I had a witness in my spirit that I was supposed to go there. He told me that he had given the letter to my classmate, Lee Morgans, but didn't know if Lee had contacted the church or not. There was a possibility that he had already been hired.

Later, when I saw Lee at Campmeeting, I asked him about the letter. He said, "Yeah, I've had this letter in my pocket since Ken Jr. gave it to me." He reached into his coat pocket and handed it to me. "I never felt led to do anything about it," he said. "I guess God was saving it for you."

I contacted the church right after Campmeeting. I went up there and preached my heart out. It didn't take much. I knew in my heart before I left Tulsa that this was the church I was supposed to pastor.

After I ministered, the congregation said they would have to fast and pray for two weeks before they would make a decision. I thought to myself, *You don't have to do that. I know I belong here.* I didn't say anything to them, though. I came back to Tulsa and told my wife to start packing. Sure enough, they called two weeks to the day and said they believed I was to be their pastor.

In both instances, I was led by an inward witness. At the first church, I had that red light, a real check in my spirit. But at the church in Minnesota, I had such peace. That is how I knew we could start packing before I had received their decision. I knew in my heart that we were supposed to be there.

Finding the Will of God

I had been in Minnesota for less than a year when, while I was praying, I perceived that I should resign my commission with the Army Reserves. At that time, I had been in the active reserves for 16 years. I only had four more years to go to retire with 20 years of service. I was a Captain at the time and was qualified for promotion up to Lt. Colonel. It looked foolish in the natural, but I had to obey God. At the next monthly meeting, I turned in my resignation.

No sooner did I do that when the Lord said, "I want you to leave the church." Well, I slipped back into the soulish realm and began to reason in my mind. You see, when I answered the call to go into full time ministry, I understood the ministry of pastor, teacher, and evangelist. I didn't understand the office of apostle or prophet, nor was I interested in either one of those offices.

I had it in my mind that I would pastor 20 years before I began to travel. At that time, I did not understand that I was in the apostolic ministry. I didn't know that apostles don't stay in one place for very long or that they build up a ministry and then turn it over to somebody else. We had started with 12 people in that church and ended up with around 80 people in nine months time. That was pretty good growth. We had no reason to leave in the natural.

When I told my wife, she did not have the same witness. I was actually relieved. I thought we were going to stay in Minnesota for awhile. A few weeks later, however, she started talking about moving. She had an inward witness that it was time for us to leave too.

At the next church business meeting, we announced that we would be leaving. We didn't have any explanation other than the Holy Spirit told us to do it. After we gave them time to find another pastor, we put our belongings in storage and packed up our station wagon. What a sight we were!

During my first experience of being led by the Spirit, I knew when I got to a city if I was supposed to be there or not. So I was trying to pick up in my spirit where we were supposed to go now. I thought it could be Boise, Idaho. We drove there and that wasn't it. From Boise we drove to Montana. From Montana we went to New Mexico; and from New Mexico, we ended up at Campmeeting in Tulsa, Oklahoma.

After Campmeeting, I decided to head back up to Minnesota. Driving through Iowa and with only had three dollars in my checking account, I was able to buy enough gas to get to Minneapolis, Minnesota. I used to teach at Alcoholics Victorious and thought that maybe I would work for them. After arriving there, however, I didn't have a witness that I was supposed to be there.

We got back into the car and headed to Willmar, Minnesota, to stay overnight with a couple that we knew from the church. When I crossed the city limits, the peace of God hit my spirit. I suddenly knew in my spirit that I was to travel full time and preach the gospel.

At first I thought this could not be God. I had pastored for less than a year. But after a little wrestling with the thought, I knew it was God. I told the Lord, "I believe this is you; and if this is you, I believe you will open the doors to preach. If the doors close, I'll get a secular job." I was looking for a way out.

When the Full Gospel Businessmen heard that I was back in town, they asked me to speak the following week. That was in 1976; and from that point on, we have always had more places to go than there is time to do it. All of this happened through an inward witness and following after peace.

Ministering Life to a Dying Woman

Here is a story where I had three different manifestations of the leading of the Holy Spirit: an inward witness, the voice of the Spirit, and an open vision.

After my family and I were back in town, I received a phone call from a young lady who had attended the church I had pastored. Her mother had been miraculously healed of cancer, six years earlier in a Kathryn Kuhlman crusade. Medical documentation confirmed it. After the woman had been healed, however, she began to attend a church that taught against the faith message. When her daughter called and asked me to go to the hospital, she said the cancer had returned. The doctors had given her mother less than two hours to live.

I arrived at the hospital to find the woman unconscious, and her eyes were glassed over. Her face looked as though death had already set in. When I went to her bedside, I knew her will was involved. I took her hand and said, "Sister, do you want to live or do you want to die? I know you can't talk, but I know you can hear me. If you want to live, squeeze my hand."

She surprised her husband and me when she said in a raspy voice, "I want to live. I do not want to die." Well, I got more than I bargained for, so I went to work. I prayed for her and declared that she would live and not die. Her daughter came to the hospital later and began to read healing scriptures to her.

After that initial visit, when I went to the hospital to visit her, I would first go to the chapel and get my instructions from the Lord. She remained unconscious. When I asked her questions, I would get quiet and listen to what the Holy Spirit impressed upon my spirit as to what her answer would be if she could speak.

I went to the hospital for the next three days. She was still on life support, but she was still alive. The two-hour death sentence had long passed. On the third day, I went to the chapel rejoicing and praising God because she was still alive. All of a sudden, it felt like somebody dumped cold water on me. At first I thought it was the devil but soon realized that it was the Holy Spirit. Then I heard the voice of the Holy Spirit—it almost sounded audible—saying "Hold fast to the confession of your faith without wavering."

Immediately, my mind visualized her dead. But in my spirit, I had an inward witness—or a perception—of what I needed to minister to her that day. First John 5:16 came to me, *"If anyone sees his brother sinning a sin which does not lead to death, he will ask, and He will give him life for those who commit sin not leading to death...."*

I didn't know what to expect as I approached her hospital room. When I walked in, everything was like it had been for the past three days. Her daughter was in the room with a friend, and they were reading healing scriptures to the girl's mother.

The mother was still unconscious. I called her by name and sat down by the side of the bed. I shared with her that the Holy Spirit impressed the scripture in 1 John 5 to minister to her. I told her that I was going to pray and ask for forgiveness on her behalf. When I said amen at the end of the prayer, a bright light went off in the room. It was like a flashbulb of a camera.

I looked at the two young ladies and their eyes were as big as saucers. They asked me, because I'm the preacher and I'm supposed to know everything, "What was that?" I didn't know, but said, "Well, there must have been a tremendous release in the spirit when I prayed." I really didn't know what I was talking about!

At seven o'clock the next morning, I received a phone call from the husband asking me to come to the hospital. I jumped in the car and quickly drove there. When I got to her room the door was closed. I checked at the nurses' station to see if I could go in and was given the go ahead.

When I stepped inside her room, her husband wasn't there; but the woman was dead. The sheet was pulled over her face and all of the machines were unhooked. It felt as though the devil had a machine gun and was rapidly shooting thoughts in my head. The thought came to me that I should be like Smith Wigglesworth and pull this lady out of her bed, stand her against the wall, and command her to live and not die. After all, she said that she did not want to die, and I had declared to everyone that she would live!

103

Of course, I also knew that if God was not in this and a nurse came in while I was dragging her body around the room, I would be locked up in the psych ward!

I had been taught to check my heart. When I did, it seemed like I could hear in my heart ever so faintly, "Don't do it." My mind, however, was screaming, "You have to do it. You said she would live and not die!" After several times of going back and forth between by head and my heart, I decided not to do anything.

To raise a person from the dead, you have to have the working of miracles, the gift of faith, and the gifts of healing in manifestation. I have since learned that if you have to stop and think about it, it is not God. When the gift of faith drops on you, there is nothing to think about. You react so quickly that everything is over before you realize what happened.

When I returned home, I got on my knees. I had questions for God, but before I could ask anything, I heard the voice of the Holy Spirit on the inside of me say, "Would you like to know what the bright light was?" I had never thought of asking that question. At that point, I was too busy thinking about my own self-preservation. Everybody in this small town thought I was either crazy or a cult. They knew I declared that this woman would live and not die.

In my heart I asked, "What was it?"

"It was me," He said. "I appeared to her, and she changed her will and decided to come home."

This lady had been married twice. During her first marriage, she suffered a lot of abuse. Now she was fighting cancer for a second time and was in a lot of pain. You can't blame her for changing her will. It was too early for her to go home. She was only in her mid-fifties, but she got tired and decided to go home early.

I thought to myself, *Fine, you've left me holding the bag.* Then I had an open vision. The room turned into a beach, and I saw a large body of water. I heard a shout for help and saw a hand in the water. The hand disappeared but then came back up again, and I heard somebody shouting for help.

Then I had a knowing on the inside of me of what this vision meant. The Holy Spirit impressed on my spirit, "When someone is in the middle of the lake drowning, it is too late to shout swimming instructions from the shore." I immediately knew what He was talking about. The woman had been miraculously healed six years before at a Kathryn Kuhlman crusade. She had six years to learn how to swim, or how to walk by faith.

Six months before she ended up in the hospital, her daughter asked if I would come to their house to pray for her. I did, but she did not receive her healing. When I visited her in the hospital, she was on the brink of death. We were trying to give her "swimming lessons" from her bedside; but in the process, she was swallowing half the lake. She was swallowing a lot of pain. You see, when someone is in the middle of the lake drowning, it is too late to shout instructions to the person on how to build his or her faith.

The Holy Spirit then reminded me to hold fast to my confession of faith without wavering. Now I knew what He was talking about. The fact that she went home to be with the Lord did not change the Word—by His stripes, you are healed (1 Pe. 2:24). I knew I was to keep preaching the healing message. This woman's death did not nullify the Word of God.

These are only a few examples of how I was led by the Holy Spirit. You can apply these examples to your family situations, jobs, businesses, and anything you are dealing with in life. It is the same Holy Spirit. He will work with you to keep you in God's perfect will and not allow the devil to derail you. It is my prayer that as you better understand spiritology, you will have revelation and understanding of how to walk in the deep things of God and be more fruitful in your life.

12

CONCLUSION

You have been given the keys to develop a strong human spirit, and you have been shown how to overcome the reasonings of your mind and the cravings of your flesh. Now, it is time for the real you—the human spirit that lives on the inside of your flesh—to dominate your physical body and not allow your intellect to rule. In the same way that God commanded the Israelites to possess the land, you must possess your own soul and flesh.

Why? The kingdom of God is on the inside of you (Luke 17:21). You are a son or daughter of God, and all power and authority has been given to you. The world is waiting for the sons of God to be revealed in the fullness of God's power (Rom. 8:19). They are waiting for you to walk in the power of the Spirit and proclaim the Good News of the kingdom of God to them. The sick need to know that they don't have to be sick any more. The poor need to know that they don't have to be poor. Those who are chained are waiting to be loosed.

It is up to you to renew your mind to who you are in Christ and walk in the power of God. As you follow after the leadings of the Holy Spirit, you will be able to proclaim the kingdom of God to those who are around you. But to walk in this power, your flesh and soul *must* take a back seat.

Samson walked in the power of the Spirit until he allowed his flesh to rule. When he gave in to his flesh, he lost that power and became a mere man. All power in heaven and earth belongs to the body of Christ. We must rise up and walk in that power and not walk as mere men.

In these last few moments of time, it is imperative to clearly hear the voice of the Holy Spirit and take back what the devil has stolen. Not just for ourselves, but for the unsaved around us. They need to hear and see the power of God. As you quit paying attention to the physical and soulish realms and walk in the Spirit, these last days on the earth will be great and grand. It is time for the captives to be set free and for people of every nation to come to the saving knowledge of the Lord Jesus Christ.

Prayer of Salvation

God loves you and wants you to be a part of His family. Jesus said in John 3:3, *"...unless one is born again, he cannot see the kingdom of God."* You become born again by accepting the free gift of salvation that was purchased through the blood Jesus shed on the Cross of Calvary.

Ephesians 2:8-9 states: *"For by grace you have been saved through faith, and that not of yourselves; it is the gift of God, not of works, lest anyone should boast."* You cannot "earn" salvation; you "receive" it by accepting Jesus Christ as your Lord and Savior.

We are told in Romans 10:9-10 that *"...if you confess with your mouth the Lord Jesus and believe in your heart that God has raised Him from the dead, you will be saved. For with the heart one believes unto righteousness and with the mouth confession is made unto salvation."* If you would like to receive Jesus into your heart, say the following prayer:

"Heavenly Father, I recognize and admit that I am a sinner. I believe that Jesus died on the cross to save me from eternal damnation. I turn away from sin and accept His free gift of salvation. I thank you that the blood of Jesus cleanses me from all unrighteousness. I declare that I am part of the family of God. Amen."

If you have prayed this prayer for the first time, please contact:
AFCM International
PO Box 1918•Willmar, MN 56201
tel. (320) 235-3838 • fax (320) 235-1802
www.afcminternational.org

About the Author

Dr. Julius "Jim" Kaseman is a graduate of the 1975 charter class of Rhema Bible Training Center in Broken Arrow, Oklahoma. In 1994, an honorary Doctor of Divinity degree was conferred upon him by Dr. R.E. Anderson from the School of Bible Theology in San Jacinto, California. He received a Bachelor of Science degree from Minot State University, Minot, North Dakota, in 1970. He also served in the United States Army and completed his military career as an Engineer Officer.

Dr. Kaseman holds credentials with Rhema Ministerial Association International and the Association of Faith Churches and Ministers and is a member of the Fellowship of Inner-City Word of Faith Ministries.

In 1975, Dr. Kaseman entered full time ministry when he accepted the invitation to pastor a church in Minnesota. A year later he was called to the traveling/teaching ministry. As a result, Jim Kaseman Ministries was founded and became instrumental in starting 27 churches in Minnesota, Iowa, South Dakota, and Montana.

The Association of Faith Churches and Ministers (AFCM) was founded in 1978. Its purpose is to promote fellowship among ministers who share Dr. Kaseman's vision of taking the "Word of Faith" message to the world. With membership now over 1,000 worldwide, AFCM continues to grow each year and provide opportunities for fellowship, strengthening, unification, and edification. AFCM also has offices in Canada and Australia.

AFCM International and AFCM Australia have translated and printed over 6 million Kenneth E. Hagin books in six different languages, which include Russian, Finnish, Estonian, Hebrew, Chinese, and Arabic.

With the aim of impacting the world with the gospel, AFCM International Training Center was founded in the fall of 1998. Since that time, hundreds of video Bible schools have been established around the world. AFCMITC is helping to fulfill the vision of AFCM/ Jim Kaseman Ministries to reach the world with the Gospel of Jesus Christ.

In addition to his responsibilities with AFCM, Dr. Kaseman ministers in churches, conventions, and Bible schools. He and his wife, Kathleen, have traveled to over 30 countries obeying God's call to go to the nations. Having seen in his own life the transforming power of the Word of God, he is committed to the presentation of the gospel in simplicity with joy and love.

Dr. Kaseman and his wife have been married for over 40 years and have five children, twelve grandchildren, and one great grandson.

To contact Dr. Kaseman

please write to:

ASSOCIATION OF FAITH
CHURCHES AND MINISTERS
INTERNAITONAL

AFCM International
PO Box 1918 • Willmar, MN 56201
tel. (320) 235-3838 • fax (320) 235-1802
www.afcminternational.org

Please include your prayers requests
and comments when you write.

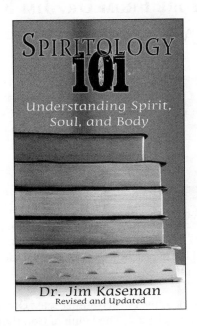

To order additional copies of *Spiritology 101: Understanding Spirit, Soul, and Body*, please write to:

AFCM International

P.O. Box 1918

Willmar, MN 56201

Or call:

(320) 235-3838

Or visit us online at:

www.afcminternational.org

Spiritology 101 is also available on CD and DVD.

6-CD set: $30.00
6-DVD set: $45.00

More From Dr. Jim Kaseman:
A Covenant of Love

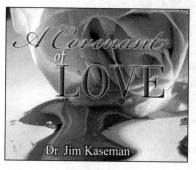

II Corinthians 5:18-19 tells us that God loves us so much that He, through His Son, Jesus Christ, laid His life on the altar of the cross so that He could reconcile us back to Himself.

Proverbs 29:29 (AMP) says that without redemptive revelation of God, the people perish. In order to walk in the fullness of all that God has provided for us, we must have a clear understanding of the New Blood Covenant.

This timely series covers such subjects as: One Everlasting Covenant; What Abraham Believed; The Lamb of God that Ratified the Abrahamic Covenant; Is Abraham's Bosom still Open?; Do Jews get a Second Chance to Get Born Again?; The Real Israel within Israel; and much more.

To order *A Covenant of Love*, please write to:

AFCM International

P.O. Box 1918

Willmar, MN 56201

Or call:

(320) 235-3838

Or visit us online at:

www.afcminternational.org

A Covenant of Love is available on CD and DVD.

6-CD set: $30.00
6-DVD set: $45.00

To Drink or Not to Drink

God tells us to study to show ourselves approved, rightly dividing the Word of Truth (II Timothy 2:15). In doing so, we will see that there is no need to be confused over this issue.

God's moral standards will become very clear regarding alcohol as Jim takes an in-depth look into the Hebrew and Greek words translated "wine."

REDEMPTION REVEALED

In this series you will discover that the Gospel of Jesus Christ was introduced to Adam and Eve, Noah, Abraham, and all of the people who have lived in the past 6000 years.

After Adam committed high treason, God announced that He would send His Son, the Second Adam, to take man's place (Genesis 3:15). What God was doing was cutting covenant with His Son. It was a covenant that could not be broken—an everlasting covenant.

Everything God promised Abraham—that he would be a great nation, a blessing to nations, and that he would inherit the land in Israel—was all promised to His Son, Jesus.

The scriptures clearly reveal that the church—the remnant, the olive tree, the living temple of God, the body of Jesus Christ—are all synonymous with Spiritual Israel. Consequently, we, the church, are joint heirs with Christ and inherit all that was promised to Jesus.

Your outlook on the Old and New Covenants will change as redemption is revealed.

To order *Redemption Revealed* please write to:

AFCM International
P.O. Box 1918
Willmar, MN 56201

Or call:
(320) 235-3838

Or visit us online at:
www.afcminternational.org

Redemption Revealed is available on CD and DVD.
10-CD set: $45.00
5(10 Sessions)-DVD set: $60.00